Living Well with Cyclothymic Disorder

A Plain-Language Guide to Understanding, Managing, and Building Long-Term Stability

Hubert Daniel McCabe

The content of this book is provided for general informational and educational purposes only. It is not intended to serve as medical advice, clinical diagnosis, or a substitute for professional assessment or treatment by a qualified health care provider. Readers should not apply any information in this book to their own situation without first consulting a licensed clinician.

All case illustrations in this book are composite and fictional. Names, identifying details, and scenarios have been created or substantially altered. Any resemblance to specific living individuals is coincidental and unintended. No case in this book is intended to represent, identify, or comment on any real person or entity.

The author and publisher make no representations or warranties of any kind, express or implied, about the completeness or accuracy of the information provided. The reader assumes full responsibility for any decisions made in reliance on the content of this book. Individual circumstances vary, and no course of reading can substitute for personalised professional care.

First Edition, 2026.

ISBN: 978-1-7648501-8-6

Table of Contents

Preface

Cyclothymia sits at a precise and frequently misread position within the bipolar spectrum. The condition is defined by the persistent cycling of mood between a hypomanic-like state and a depressive-like state across a minimum of two years, with no single episode reaching the severity or duration required for a diagnosis of hypomania or major depression. This distinction, between sub-threshold episodes and the full clinical presentations that define bipolar I and bipolar II disorder, is both the source of cyclothymia's specificity as a diagnosis and the reason it is so consistently misidentified.

The research record on cyclothymia is clear on several points that have not reached popular or clinical awareness at scale. Cyclothymia is a primary mood disorder with documented genetic loading, neurobiological correlates in circadian rhythm dysregulation, and a progression risk toward full bipolar disorder that ranges across studies from 15 to 50 percent when the condition is left unmanaged. The episode threshold is sub-threshold. The functional impact across a life is not. People with cyclothymia experience clinically significant impairment in occupational functioning, in their capacity to sustain relationships, and in their sense of self-consistency, and they experience this impairment across years, not across discrete episodes.

The gap this creates is specific. People who receive a cyclothymia diagnosis typically arrive at it after years of partial treatment, most commonly with antidepressants prescribed for the depressive component without the cycling structure being identified or addressed. They may have been told they have recurrent depression, generalised anxiety, or a personality disorder, each of which captures one feature of the presentation while missing the cyclothymic pattern that organises the whole. Even those who reach the correct diagnosis encounter very limited consumer-level literature explaining what the condition means, what drives it biologically, and what the current evidence base recommends for management.

This book is a clinical psychoeducation guide written for a general readership. It draws on the social zeitgeber model of mood cycling, the interpersonal and social rhythm therapy framework developed by Frank and colleagues, and the current consensus on pharmacological management in cyclothymia to provide a structured account of the condition in plain-language consumer format. It is organised around understanding before application: the chapters on what cyclothymia is, how it is diagnosed, and what drives the cycling biologically precede the chapters on management. The reasoning behind each treatment approach is explained, not simply recommended.

The book is a standalone title. Companion workbooks in the Theo Press clinical catalogue address structured skill-building; this guide provides the explanatory foundation that precedes that work and can be read independently of it.

The book is written primarily for adults who have received a cyclothymia diagnosis or who have a mood history that the diagnosis may explain. Partners, family members, and practitioners will find the content directly relevant to their own understanding of the condition. What the book is not is a clinical assessment, a prescribing guide, or a substitute for the individualised judgment of a qualified clinician. The case illustrations throughout are composite and fictional, created to make clinical concepts concrete rather than to represent any identifiable person or situation. No outcome is promised or implied.

The framework is practical. The aim is clarity.

Introduction

You probably tried to explain it a hundred times, in different rooms, to different people. To a GP who offered you an antidepressant prescription and a leaflet about sleep hygiene. To a therapist who said you seemed "resilient" when you were in the room and "difficult" when you weren't. To a partner who loved you but couldn't understand why the person who had been intensely present, full of plans, unable to stop talking, had become someone who barely got out of bed by Thursday. Maybe you tried explaining it to yourself, with a succession of self-diagnoses that each fit partially but never entirely. Depression? That covered the lows but ignored the highs. Bipolar disorder? The descriptions felt too extreme, too episodic, too dramatic for what you actually experienced. Anxiety? That was part of it but not the whole picture.

The years of not having a name for it cost something real. People with cyclothymia report diagnostic delays averaging many years, during which they may receive several incorrect diagnoses, undergo treatment that does not fit their actual condition, and carry a private conviction that something fundamental is wrong without any framework for understanding what (Bielecki & Gupta, 2023). That conviction is accurate. The framework has simply been missing.

Cyclothymia is a mood disorder on the bipolar spectrum. It is characterized by cycling periods of hypomanic symptoms, elevated mood and energy that does not reach the full threshold for a hypomanic episode, and depressive symptoms that do not reach the full threshold for major depression. The cycling continues for at least two years in adults, present for more than half the time, with no symptom-free gap exceeding two months (American Psychiatric Association, 2022). That clinical description does not capture how it feels to live inside it. What it feels like is a mood that never holds still. Good periods that tip into too much. Low periods that arrive without warning and stay without reason. A sense of being out of step with your own life.

This guide was written for the reader who has, recently or finally, been given the cyclothymia diagnosis. It is also for the reader who suspects the diagnosis and has not yet had it confirmed. And it is for partners and family members trying to understand what the person they care about is actually experiencing.

What this book is not is a workbook. There is one dedicated workbook on cyclothymia in consumer publishing, published in 2005, and it remains useful. This is something different. This is the guide you read to understand the condition before, or alongside, any exercises or therapeutic work. Think of it as the clinical friend who explains the whole picture rather than jumping straight to homework.

The book moves from understanding to application. The early chapters cover what cyclothymia is, why it was so hard to diagnose, and how to begin reading your own cycles. The middle chapters cover the evidence base for treatment: social rhythm therapy, sleep, medication, and psychological approaches. The later chapters cover the daily reality of living with cyclothymia across relationships, work, and comorbid conditions. The final chapter helps you build a personal stability framework.

Throughout, three themes run like threads. The first is that cyclothymia is a genuine, specific condition with its own biology, its own pattern, and its own treatment principles. It is not mild bipolar disorder, and it is not a personality trait. The second is that stability is achievable, not as a permanent flattening of your mood but as a relationship with your cycling brain that becomes, over time, less costly. The third is that the treatments that work are not always the ones you have already tried.

Before reading Chapter 1, take a moment to write a single sentence about the experience that first made you wonder whether the word "cyclothymia" might apply to you. Keep it somewhere you can find it when you reach the conclusion. The difference between what you write now and how you think about that experience by the end of the book is part of what this guide is for.

Chapter 1: What Cyclothymia Actually Is

The single most common thing clinicians and writers say about cyclothymia is that it is a mild form of bipolar disorder. This framing has been repeated so often, by so many people who should know better, that it has become background noise in clinical settings and online health guides alike. It is also wrong in ways that damage the lives of the people it gets applied to.

Cyclothymia is not mild bipolar disorder. It is a distinct condition on the bipolar spectrum with its own clinical character, its own diagnostic criteria, its own trajectory, and its own treatment considerations. The word "mild" refers only to the intensity of individual episodes, not to the severity of disruption the condition produces across a life. That distinction matters enormously, and this chapter makes it precisely, because everything that follows depends on understanding what cyclothymia actually is.

The Condition in Plain Terms

Cyclothymia, also called cyclothymic disorder, is a primary mood disorder characterized by chronic, fluctuating instability between two mood states: a hypomanic-like state, in which mood and energy are elevated above the person's baseline, and a depressive-like state, in which mood and energy fall below it. Neither state, at the level of individual episodes, reaches the clinical threshold for a full hypomanic episode or a major depressive episode. But both states are real, disruptive, and persistent (American Psychiatric Association, 2022).

The defining feature of cyclothymia is not the depth of any particular trough or the height of any particular peak. It is the chronicity of the cycling itself. A person with cyclothymia will experience these mood fluctuations for at least two years, present for more than 50 percent of the time, with no stable period exceeding two months. The mood has barely settled before it moves again. This is what gives cyclothymia its functional weight: not a single catastrophic episode but the accumulated cost of a mood that never lets you land.

Estimates of how many people have cyclothymia range from 0.4 to 1 percent of the general population, though researchers widely believe these figures are conservative given the disorder's chronic underdiagnosis (Cleveland Clinic, 2022). The condition typically appears in late childhood or adolescence, affects men and women in roughly equal proportions, and is classified under bipolar and related disorders in the DSM-5-TR (American Psychiatric Association, 2022). It is not a transient condition. Without treatment, it tends to continue indefinitely, and for between 15 and 50 percent of people with cyclothymia, it eventually progresses to a full diagnosis of bipolar I or bipolar II disorder (Perugi et al., 2017a).

What the Diagnosis Actually Requires

The DSM-5-TR lists four criteria for cyclothymic disorder. Understanding them in plain language is worth doing carefully, because misunderstanding them is one reason the diagnosis gets missed.

Criterion A states that for at least two years (one year in children and adolescents), a person has experienced numerous periods of hypomanic symptoms that do not meet the full criteria for a hypomanic episode, alternating with numerous periods of depressive symptoms that do not meet the full criteria for a major depressive episode.

The key phrase here is "numerous periods." Cyclothymia is not diagnosed on the basis of one or two instances of feeling unusually energetic or unusually flat. The cycling must be a persistent, recurring pattern across years, not months.

Criterion B states that during the two-year period, the hypomanic and depressive symptoms have been present for at least half of the time, and that the person has not been without symptoms for more than two consecutive months.

This criterion is the diagnostic signature of cyclothymia. Unlike episodic mood disorders, where discrete episodes occur against a background of normal functioning, cyclothymia creates a state of near-continuous mood instability. The stable windows, when they occur, are brief. Most are shorter than eight weeks.

Criterion C states that the full criteria for a hypomanic, manic, or major depressive episode have never been met.

This is the criterion that distinguishes cyclothymia from bipolar I and bipolar II. If a person has ever had a full manic episode, the diagnosis is bipolar I. If a person has ever had a full hypomanic episode alongside a past major depressive episode, the diagnosis is bipolar II. Cyclothymia occupies the space below those thresholds, not because the symptoms are minor in their impact, but because they do not reach specific clinical severity or duration markers that define those higher-threshold episodes.

Criterion D states that the symptoms cause clinically significant distress or impairment in social, occupational, or other important areas of functioning.

This criterion refutes, in the DSM's own language, the idea that cyclothymia is subclinical. It does not qualify as a diagnosis unless the cycling produces real disruption to a real life. The word "mild" in the lay framing of cyclothymia describes the episode threshold, not the functional outcome.

Sub-threshold Does Not Mean Sub-impact

The distinction between sub-threshold episodes and sub-impact experience is one of the most important concepts in understanding cyclothymia, and it is almost universally missed in popular descriptions of the condition.

When researchers and clinicians describe cyclothymia's episodes as sub-threshold, they mean only that the individual hypomanic or depressive periods do not meet the duration or severity criteria for full episodes as defined by DSM-5-TR. A full hypomanic episode, for example, requires at least four consecutive days of elevated, expansive, or irritable mood with increased activity. A major depressive episode requires at least two consecutive weeks of five or more specified symptoms. The episodes in cyclothymia fall short of these duration thresholds, and individual symptoms may be less severe.

What this classification does not capture is the cumulative impact of living in a near-continuous state of mood instability for years. The Merck Manual notes directly that "living with cyclothymic disorder is not easy because interpersonal relationships are often stormy" (Merck Manual Professional Edition, 2024). Cyclothymia has been linked to poor work performance, high rates of relationship breakdown, social anxiety, fear of rejection, and significant occupational impairment (Perugi et al., 2017a). The condition also carries elevated rates of suicidal ideation even in its "mild" form.

The reason this matters clinically is that if a provider treats cyclothymia as though it is sub-impact because it is sub-threshold, they will undertreat it. That undertreatment increases the risk of progression to bipolar I or II, the risk of antidepressant-driven destabilization, and the accumulation of life damage that happens while the real diagnosis waits.

The Cyclothymic Character

Cyclothymia has a clinical character that makes it recognizable beyond its formal diagnostic criteria. Understanding this character can help readers recognize their own experience and distinguish it from conditions with which cyclothymia is commonly confused.

The first feature is **early onset**. Cyclothymia typically begins in late childhood or adolescence, meaning that for most adults with the diagnosis, the cycling mood has been present since before they had adult language for what was happening to them. Many describe feeling "always like this" in a way that made them assume the instability was simply their personality.

The second feature is **emotional reactivity and interpersonal sensitivity**. People with cyclothymia tend to respond to interpersonal events with mood shifts that others experience as disproportionate. A perceived criticism, a social slight, an ambiguous text message can trigger a shift downward that then takes days to recover from. This is not a character flaw. It is a feature of the cyclothymic temperament that reflects the underlying mood regulation difficulty and has been documented consistently in the research literature (Akiskal & Pinto, 1999).

The third feature is **impulsivity**, which tends to be most pronounced during hypomanic-like phases. Impulsive spending, impulsive social commitments, impulsive relationship decisions, impulsive career moves made from a position of elevated certainty that quickly passes. The impulsivity is not random; it follows the cycle.

The fourth feature is **creative and interpersonal intensity** during elevated phases. This is the feature that makes cyclothymia feel, at times, like an asset. The surge of energy and ideas during a hypomanic-like phase can produce genuine creative output, social vitality, and periods of exceptional productivity. The cost comes when the phase ends and the commitments, decisions, and relationships made during it have to be maintained from a depleted baseline.

The fifth feature is **cyclothymia's reactivity**, meaning that mood shifts can be triggered by relatively minor environmental events. Jet lag, a disrupted night's sleep, a stressful week at work, a significant life change: any of these can push the system into a phase shift. Chapter 5 covers the biology and triggers in detail.

A Disorder, Not a Personality

One of the most common experiences reported by people with cyclothymia is the sense that the condition has been absorbed into their identity before it was recognized as a condition. Because cyclothymia begins early and because its episodes are sub-threshold, it tends to be experienced, and described to others, as simply how a person is. Moody. Intense. Hard to live with. Brilliant but unreliable. These characterizations substitute for a clinical understanding of what is actually happening.

The research is clear that cyclothymia is a mood disorder with a biological substrate, not a personality configuration. It has genetic components: family history of bipolar disorder or cyclothymia significantly increases risk (Bielecki & Gupta, 2023). It has neurobiological correlates in serotonergic and dopaminergic dysregulation, circadian rhythm abnormalities, and stress responsiveness. It responds to treatments that target mood regulation, not personality restructuring.

This does not mean the person with cyclothymia is "not responsible" for their behavior during episodes. It means that their behavior during episodes is shaped by a mood state that is not fully under voluntary control, and that treatment can substantially alter that mood state. Recognizing the disorder for what it is, a treatable medical condition, is the prerequisite for accessing that treatment.

Case 1: Arden

The following is a composite illustration. Details have been changed and identifying information removed.

Background: Arden, a 34-year-old project manager, was referred for a psychiatric assessment following her third resignation from a senior role in five years. Each resignation had followed the same pattern: a period of exceptional performance, visibility, and productivity during which she took on more than any colleague, followed by a period of poor attendance, missed deadlines, and withdrawal from team relationships. Arden described these patterns as "just how I work" and initially resisted the referral.

Presentation: Assessment revealed a two-year-plus history of recurring mood periods. During elevated phases, lasting days to two weeks, Arden reported reduced sleep need (four to five hours felt sufficient), racing thoughts that she experienced as clarity, strong social confidence, heightened libido, and a drive to initiate multiple new projects. During low phases, she described exhaustion, difficulty with basic decisions, anhedonia, and an inability to respond to messages she described as feeling "two feet thick."

Analysis: The individual elevated periods did not meet full criteria for a hypomanic episode in terms of duration or impairment marker (Arden continued working through most of them). The individual low periods fell short of major depression criteria for symptom count and duration. The two-year cycling pattern, present for more than 50 percent of the time, with no gap exceeding eight weeks, met criteria for cyclothymia under DSM-5-TR. Previous clinicians had documented MDD (treated twice with SSRIs, both times with limited benefit and one episode of increased agitation) and adjustment disorder.

Intervention: Arden was started on a low dose of lamotrigine, referred for IPSRT, and provided with psychoeducation about cyclothymia's occupational impact. Mood tracking was introduced.

Outcome: Over six months, Arden had not resigned from her current role. She described her mood as "narrower" and reported that she was beginning to recognize phase shifts before they fully arrived. She expressed frustration that the correct diagnosis had taken twelve years.

Teaching Points:

- Cyclothymia can produce significant occupational impairment without any single episode reaching full diagnostic threshold.

- SSRI use without mood stabilization can worsen cycling in cyclothymia (discussed in Chapter 8).

- Early cycling patterns visible in retrospect across the person's employment history can be clinically informative.

Case 2: Bellamy and Calloway (Braided)

Both are composite illustrations.

Bellamy was referred following a three-week period of elevated mood, reduced sleep, increased social activity, and spending that exceeded their monthly income. Their partner described them as "a completely different person" during this period, charismatic and confident in ways that alarmed rather than attracted. The episode ended abruptly, and Bellamy spent the following three weeks in bed. Assessment revealed this was a first recognized full hypomanic episode. A past major depressive episode was documented. Diagnosis: bipolar II disorder.

Calloway presented with similar chief complaint: mood swings disrupting their work and relationship. Their elevated periods, however, lasted three to five days rather than weeks, with symptoms present but not at the level their partner noticed as dramatic or alarming. Low periods lasted a similar duration. The pattern had repeated, with minimal breaks, for three years. No episode met full criteria for hypomania or major depression. Assessment also revealed elevated interpersonal sensitivity and a history going back to adolescence. Diagnosis: cyclothymic disorder.

Both disorders involve cycling between elevated and depressive states. Both can produce substantial life disruption. The clinical distinction lies in the episode structure: Bellamy's episodes meet the four-day minimum for hypomania and the two-week minimum for major depression. Calloway's do not. The treatment implications differ significantly, covered in Chapters 8 and 9.

What to Carry Forward

Twelve years after her first MDD diagnosis, Arden finally had a name for what had been disrupting her career. The mood tracking she started in week two of treatment showed a pattern immediately recognizable in retrospect: the four-day elevated window, the eight to ten-day low, the brief return to baseline, then the cycle again. She said, later, that seeing it charted was less frightening than she expected. The pattern had been there the whole time. Now she could see it.

Cyclothymia is a real condition with documented biology, documented functional impact, and documented treatments that work. The episode threshold is sub-threshold. The life impact is not. The word "mild" belongs only to the individual episode, not to the years of living inside the cycling. Carrying this distinction into every subsequent chapter is the foundation everything else rests on.

Chapter 2: The Long Road to Diagnosis

In 1921, Emil Kraepelin described what he called "the fundamental states" of manic-depressive illness: mood states that did not reach full episode threshold but represented a persistent constitutional tendency toward cycling. He included among these what he termed "cyclothymic temperament," and he argued, against the prevailing view of his time, that these temperamental variants were continuous with the major mood disorders rather than separate from them. For most of the twentieth century, psychiatry did not follow him there.

The field moved instead toward categorical diagnosis: discrete episodes with clear start and end points, separable from underlying personality and temperament. Cyclothymia was recognized as a category in the DSM-III in 1980, but it occupied an uncertain space, often classified as a personality disorder, rarely seen as a clinical priority, and consistently undertreated. It was not until Hagop Akiskal's systematic work on the bipolar spectrum in the 1970s and 1980s that cyclothymia was repositioned as an affective disorder with genuine biological continuity with the bipolar spectrum (Akiskal et al., 1977). Even that repositioning took decades to reach clinical practice. Most practicing clinicians today were trained in systems that treated cyclothymia as peripheral.

This history matters because it explains something the reader with cyclothymia almost certainly experienced firsthand: the diagnosis takes a very long time to arrive.

Why the Diagnosis Gets Missed

Cyclothymia is underdiagnosed for reasons that are structural rather than negligent, though the structural reasons can feel negligent when you are living through them.

The first reason is presentation pattern. Most people with cyclothymia seek help during a depressive phase, not during an elevated phase. This is entirely rational: the low feels bad and motivates help-seeking; the high often feels good, or at least productive, and does not prompt a clinical encounter. A clinician who sees only the depressive presentation, without probing for elevated periods, will reach for a depression diagnosis. Many do.

The second reason is the sub-threshold quality of the episodes. Because the elevated periods in cyclothymia do not meet the four-day minimum for hypomania and the depressive periods do not meet the two-week minimum or five-symptom count for major depression, a clinician applying strict DSM episode criteria may examine each episode individually and conclude that no episode-level diagnosis applies. The two-year pattern that would yield the cyclothymia diagnosis requires a longitudinal view that a single assessment rarely provides.

The third reason is diagnostic confusion with other conditions. Cyclothymia shares features with several conditions that are more commonly recognized. Borderline personality disorder and cyclothymia both involve emotional lability, impulsivity, and interpersonal sensitivity, and the two are frequently confused, especially in adolescents and young adults. Both major depressive disorder and cyclothymia involve recurring depressive symptoms. Both generalized anxiety disorder and cyclothymia involve chronic dysphoria and a sense of unease that is hard to locate precisely. Attention deficit hyperactivity disorder and cyclothymia share impulsivity and difficulty with sustained attention, and the two frequently co-occur. Any of these diagnoses can be made and treated while the underlying cyclothymic pattern goes unnamed.

The fourth reason is clinician awareness. Cyclothymia is underrepresented in clinical training curricula. A 2023 clinical review described it as a disorder that "presents a challenge for the clinician as many patients present with non-specific symptoms and may be mistaken for similarly manifesting psychiatric disorders" (Bielecki & Gupta, 2023). Clinicians who are less familiar with the diagnostic criteria, or who hold the misperception that cyclothymia is too mild to warrant significant clinical attention, may not include it in their differential diagnosis even when the pattern is present.

The Misdiagnosis Maze

The specific misdiagnoses that precede a cyclothymia diagnosis are not random. They follow a pattern that reflects both the clinical presentation of cyclothymia and the biases of the diagnostic system.

Major depressive disorder is the most common preceding diagnosis. The depressive phase of cyclothymia is real, functionally impairing, and often indistinguishable in a cross-sectional assessment from an episode of MDD. If the clinician does not ask about elevated periods, does not probe for hypomanic features in the history, or does not notice that the "MDD" has responded poorly to antidepressants and may even have been worsened by them, the cycling pattern goes undetected.

Borderline personality disorder is a particularly problematic misdiagnosis for cyclothymia because the treatment approaches for the two conditions diverge in significant ways. BPD-oriented treatment focuses on attachment patterns, identity disturbance, and emotion regulation from a relational and developmental perspective. Cyclothymia requires mood stabilization as a primary foundation. A person with cyclothymia who receives years of BPD treatment, without their mood disorder being addressed, is receiving incomplete care (Perugi et al., 2017a). The confusion arises because both conditions involve emotional reactivity, impulsivity, and relational turbulence. The key distinguishing features are the episodic quality of cyclothymia's mood states (which shift in cycles rather than being continuously dysregulated) and the absence of the identity disturbance and frantic avoidance of abandonment that are central to BPD.

Bipolar I or II is sometimes assigned when a clinician overestimates episode severity or duration. The inverse error, underestimating the episode and missing bipolar I or II when it is actually present, is more common, but the diagnosis of cyclothymia can itself be missed in either direction.

Getting to the Right Answer

Cyclothymia diagnosis requires a longitudinal view of mood history that most initial clinical encounters do not provide. This means that readers who are pursuing or who have recently received the diagnosis may need to be active participants in the assessment process in ways that feel unusual.

A clinician conducting a thorough assessment for cyclothymia will ask about mood history across years, not just current or recent episodes. They will probe for elevated periods specifically: times of reduced sleep with sustained energy, periods of unusual productivity or talkativeness, episodes of increased impulsivity or goal-directed activity. They will ask about the patterning of these periods over time, whether they recur, how long they last, what brings them on. They will review past treatment responses, particularly responses to antidepressants, which can be informative about underlying bipolar-spectrum pathology.

If you are approaching an assessment having already done some research, or having received previous diagnoses that did not fit, it is clinically helpful to arrive with a documented mood history. This can be as simple as a handwritten timeline of significant mood episodes across your adult life, with approximate dates, durations, and what was happening at the time. Chapter 3 covers mood tracking in detail; that framework can also be applied retrospectively to construct this kind of history.

Case 1: Cypress

A composite narrative.

Cypress was thirty-one when a trainee psychiatrist asked, almost as an afterthought, whether there had been periods of feeling "the opposite of how you feel now." Not just neutral, not fine, but actually better than usual. More energy than made sense. Less need for sleep. Ideas that came faster than normal.

Cypress had to think about it. The question had never been asked before, across nine years of MDD treatment and two courses of SSRIs that had worked partially, briefly, and then seemed to stop working, or to make things worse in ways that were hard to describe.

Yes, Cypress said. There had been those periods. They lasted a few days, usually. Sometimes a couple of weeks. During them, Cypress felt capable of things they didn't normally feel capable of. They'd written a third of a novel in ten days one March, then not been able to open the file for four months. They'd applied for three jobs in a single weekend during a period like that, got interviews for two, and felt utterly incapable of preparing for either by the time the dates arrived.

The trainee psychiatrist spent another forty minutes taking a mood history. At the end of it, the senior clinician they consulted said: cyclothymia. Probably since the mid-twenties. Possibly earlier.

Cypress's response, they later reported, was not relief exactly. It was closer to recognition. Like having named something you had been tripping over in the dark for a decade.

The first SSRI course had been prescribed for the depression. The second had been prescribed when the first stopped working. Neither had been wrong exactly, given the information available at the time. What they had missed was the cycling, and treating one half of a cycling mood disorder with a medication that can worsen cycling was leaving half the condition unaddressed. The treatment shift required a different approach, covered in Chapter 8.

Case 2: Dune

A composite labeled case.

Background: Dune, a 27-year-old in their third year of a psychology degree, was referred for assessment after expressing concern about their BPD diagnosis, which they had received at 22. They reported that the BPD frame had never quite fit their experience of themselves, though they acknowledged shared features.

Presentation: Dune described mood instability that they experienced as cyclical rather than reactive. Their low periods arrived without obvious precipitants, lasted approximately five to twelve days, and lifted without a clear trigger. Elevated periods were shorter, two to four days, and characterized by restlessness, decreased sleep, urgency, and a sense of clarity that sometimes tipped into irritability. They described a longstanding pattern of intense connections with people that shifted when the cycle shifted.

Analysis: A structured mood history taken across four sessions revealed a cycling pattern dating to age 17. No episode met full criteria for either mania or major depression. The absence of identity disturbance and the episodic, cycling quality of the mood shifts distinguished Dune's presentation from a primary BPD diagnosis. Cyclothymia criteria were met. Comorbid social anxiety was noted.

Intervention: The treating clinician discussed both diagnoses and their overlap with Dune, using the episodic cycle as the distinguishing frame. Dune began a mood diary and was referred for IPSRT. Valproate was discussed and declined by Dune pending further psychoeducation.

Outcome: Dune reported feeling "genuinely curious, rather than frightened" about the cyclothymia frame within six weeks. They were able to trace the interpersonal ruptures in their history back through the cycle in a way that felt, they said, less shameful than the personality disorder framing had sometimes felt.

Teaching Point: Misdiagnosis is not the fault of the person who carries it. It reflects the genuine diagnostic complexity of cyclothymia and the need for a longitudinal rather than cross-sectional view of mood history.

Where This Leaves Us

Kraepelin described the cycling temperamental states in 1921. A century later, people are still spending years inside the cycling without a name for it.

The delay is not inevitable. When clinicians ask the right questions across the full mood history, including the elevated periods that often go unreported, the pattern becomes visible. The reader who has spent years being treated for half their condition, or no named condition at all, is not unusual. The path forward begins with the correct framework, which is now in your hands.

Chapter 3 moves from the history of the diagnosis to the practical skill of recognizing what the cycle actually looks and feels like, in real time, in your own experience.

Chapter 3: Reading Your Own Cycles

It is eleven-thirty on a Tuesday night and Ellis cannot sit down.

The apartment is not dirty, but Ellis has cleaned it anyway, the kind of cleaning that starts with the kitchen counter and ends with the inside of the refrigerator and a reorganized linen closet. Three tabs are open on the laptop: a job listing for a position Ellis is not currently looking for, a half-drafted email to a friend Ellis has not spoken to in two years, and a playlist of songs that Ellis keeps not quite listening to because a better playlist keeps suggesting itself. Ellis has had four hours of sleep in the past two nights and does not feel tired. Ellis feels, in fact, like something that needs to happen, though exactly what is unclear.

This will not last. In five days, or seven, or ten, Ellis will feel the opposite of this. Not tired exactly, though tired will be part of it. More like the opposite of necessary. The apartment will look fine; cleaning it will feel like a project requiring resources that are not there. The email will go unsent. The job listing will be forgotten. The playlist will be too much effort.

Ellis has been here before. Many times. What Ellis has not had, until recently, is a name for where "here" actually is.

The Hypomanic Phase Up Close

What Ellis was experiencing on that Tuesday night was the hypomanic-like phase of cyclothymia. The word "hypomanic" carries the prefix hypo, meaning below or under, in this case below the level of a full manic episode. Understanding what hypomania feels like from the inside matters because it is the feature of cyclothymia that is most frequently missed, most easily mistaken for normal mood variation, and most often responsible for the misdiagnosis of pure depression.

During a hypomanic-like phase, the predominant experience is typically one or more of the following: elevated mood, meaning a sense of buoyancy or well-being that exceeds what the circumstances warrant; **irritable elevated mood**, which is hypomania experienced not as happiness but as a pressured, easily-triggered agitation; and increased energy or goal-directed activity, the sense that things must be started, done, initiated, completed.

Associated features include reduced need for sleep without daytime fatigue, which is distinct from insomnia (the person feels rested on fewer hours, or does not notice tiredness even when awake long into the night); racing thoughts or flight of ideas; increased talkativeness or pressure of speech; distractibility; and impulsivity, particularly around spending, social commitments, sexual behavior, or ambitious planning.

In cyclothymia specifically, the elevated periods are sub-threshold in the sense that they do not meet the four-day minimum for a full hypomanic episode, though they may last several days, and they may or may not produce the level of observable behavioral change that prompts others to notice. What varies significantly between people is which symptoms predominate. Some cyclothymia patients primarily experience the elevated mood and creative surge. Others primarily experience the irritable, pressured form, which is less recognizable as a "high" and may present as anger, intolerance, or what gets described as "being difficult."

One feature that distinguishes cyclothymia's elevated phases from ordinary good moods is the quality of the change from baseline. In cyclothymia, the elevated period represents a departure from how the person usually functions: more energetic than usual, not just more energetic than yesterday. The person and those around them often recognize it as a different state. The difficulty is that, from the inside, it can feel like the true self, the capable and alive version, rather than a symptomatic state.

The Low Phase Up Close

The depressive phase of cyclothymia shares surface features with major depressive disorder: low mood, diminished energy, reduced interest in activities that are usually engaging, difficulty with concentration and decision-making, changes in sleep and appetite. The differences are primarily matters of duration and severity threshold, with cyclothymia's low phases typically lasting days to a few weeks rather than the two-week minimum for an MDD episode.

What makes the cyclothymia low phase distinct from typical depression is its cycling context. It arrives after the elevated phase, or it arrives without the elevated phase having been recognized, which means the person may experience only the crash without understanding why it happened. The low is also often characterized by a specific emptiness rather than the heavy sadness of classic depression. Anhedonia, the inability to feel pleasure in things that are usually pleasurable, can be pronounced. Physical symptoms are common: fatigue that does not improve with rest, a persistent heaviness in the limbs, headaches.

One feature consistently noted in the clinical literature on cyclothymia's depressive phases is hypersensitivity to social stimuli. The fear of rejection and the tendency to experience interpersonal events as acutely painful are intensified during the low phase. A message left on read, a slight change in a colleague's tone, a perceived coolness from a partner: these can feel catastrophic in a way that the same events do not feel during a neutral period.

Suicidal ideation is possible during cyclothymia's depressive phases. This is documented in the clinical literature and is not limited to more severe mood disorders. Anyone experiencing suicidal thoughts should contact a mental health professional or crisis service; this guide is not a substitute for that support.

The Brief Stable Window

Between the elevated and depressive phases, many people with cyclothymia experience periods of relative stability. These windows, when they occur, tend to be brief. The DSM-5-TR requires, for diagnosis, that no symptom-free period exceeds two consecutive months. Many people with cyclothymia report stable windows of days to a few weeks rather than months.

The stable window matters because it establishes what the person's baseline actually is. During periods of mood instability, it can be difficult to remember or trust the baseline. Mood tracking across time, covered below, helps establish this baseline concretely and provides a reference point for identifying when phases are beginning.

Why Cycles Can Shift Within a Day

A feature of cyclothymia that surprises many newly diagnosed readers is how rapidly mood can shift, sometimes within a single day. A morning of elevated, productive, confident energy can give way by mid-afternoon to fatigue, lowered confidence, and a pronounced sense of deflation. This within-day variability is more common in cyclothymia than in bipolar I or II, where mood states tend to persist across days, weeks, or months.

The within-day variability reflects the underlying instability of mood regulation in cyclothymia and its relationship to circadian rhythms, sleep patterns, and interpersonal events. Morning often brings the elevated phase, with energy and motivation peaking in the late morning and early afternoon. Evening tends toward the lower end, with mood dipping as the circadian system winds down. Any interpersonal stressor can shift the trajectory.

Understanding this diurnal pattern, if it applies to your experience, has practical implications. Scheduling demanding tasks for the higher-energy morning window while building in lower-demand activities for the afternoon is a practical accommodation, not an avoidance strategy.

Beginning to Track

Mood tracking is the practice of regularly recording mood state, energy level, sleep, and notable events in order to map the cycling pattern over time. It is the single most useful thing a person newly diagnosed with cyclothymia can begin doing, because it converts an experience that feels chaotic and unpredictable into something that can be observed, recognized, and eventually anticipated.

Effective mood tracking for cyclothymia does not require a sophisticated app or complex form. The minimum useful data is a twice-daily rating (morning and evening) of mood on a scale of one to ten, with five representing neutral, numbers above five representing elevated states, and numbers below five representing lower states. Adding energy level (separately from mood, since they can diverge), hours of sleep, and any notable event completes the basic data set.

The pattern typically becomes recognizable within two to four weeks of consistent tracking. What most people notice first is not the extremes but the transitions, the moments when the line on the chart begins to shift direction, which tend to correspond to recognizable physiological and behavioral changes. Those transitions are the prodromal window, the early warning period, during which intervention is most effective.

Case 2: Fable (Worked Example)

A composite worked example. Details are illustrative rather than identifying.

Fable had been tracking mood for six weeks when the pattern first became readable. The chart showed:

Weeks 1-2: Ratings clustered between 6 and 8, with energy high (7-9), sleep averaging five and a half hours, and two notations of "can't shut off" and "started three new projects."

Days 15-16: Ratings dropped sharply. Energy fell from 8 to 4 within 48 hours. Sleep jumped to nine hours but felt non-restorative.

Weeks 3-4: Ratings between 3 and 5. Energy 3-5. Sleep variable (seven to ten hours). Notations included "cancelled gym," "left work early," "couldn't return calls."

Day 29: Ratings began climbing again. Energy 5, then 6. Sleep shortened to six hours. Notation: "felt like myself for the first time in a while."

What the chart revealed was a cycle of approximately fourteen days in length: seven to ten days elevated, five to eight days low, with the transitions happening faster than Fable had recognized in real time. Fable had assumed the low phases "came out of nowhere." The chart showed they came from the high, consistently, within forty-eight hours of the ratings crossing a threshold of about 7.5 sustained across two days.

The clinically useful output of this exercise was the identification of Fable's personal early warning threshold: sustained ratings above 7 with shortened sleep were predictors of an impending low. That pattern, once recognized, allowed Fable to bring forward the protective sleep strategies covered in Chapter 7, adding them at the 7-sustained point rather than waiting for the crash.

Key Concepts Review

The cold scene at the start of this chapter was not fiction. It is the inside of a hypomanic-like phase: the energy, the plans that feel urgent, the sleep that is not needed, the tasks that multiply. That scene belongs to cyclothymia. So does the scene that follows it five or seven days later, when the apartment is fine and Ellis cannot make herself care about any of it.

Naming these phases, recognizing their quality, and tracking them consistently converts a chaotic experience into something legible. Mood tracking is not a cure, but it is the foundation on which everything else in this guide rests. Chapter 4 turns from the felt experience of the cycle to its position in the broader landscape of bipolar-spectrum disorder.

Chapter 4: Your Place on the Spectrum

Cyclothymia is on the bipolar spectrum. That is the position of the DSM-5-TR, the clinical consensus, and the research literature. Cyclothymia is also, in the view of a meaningful portion of researchers and clinicians, not really a bipolar disorder in the way that bipolar I and bipolar II are bipolar disorders. Both of these statements are true. Neither cancels the other out. And the tension between them is not a minor academic disagreement: it has direct implications for how cyclothymia is diagnosed, how it is treated, and how people with the condition understand themselves.

This chapter examines both positions, gives each its due weight, and lands where the evidence actually supports landing. For the reader with cyclothymia, the practical question is not which side of the debate wins but what the classification means for the management of a real condition in a real life.

The Spectrum Concept

The idea that mood disorders exist on a spectrum, rather than as discrete and separate categories, has a long history in psychiatry. Kraepelin positioned it there in 1921. Hagop Akiskal, working across the 1970s and 1980s, provided the systematic empirical case for what he called the "soft bipolar spectrum," a range of affective presentations below the threshold of classic bipolar I that nonetheless share biological and familial features with the higher-threshold disorders (Akiskal & Pinto, 1999).

In this spectrum model, cyclothymia sits at the lower end: above normal mood variability, below the threshold of bipolar II, sharing genetic risk factors and treatment principles with the more severe forms. The spectrum model predicts that the conditions will grade into one another, that cyclothymia carries real risk of progression to bipolar II or I, and that treatment should follow the same general principles across the spectrum: mood stabilization first, caution with antidepressants, attention to circadian regularity.

The DSM-5-TR adopted this framework by classifying cyclothymia under "Bipolar and Related Disorders," alongside bipolar I and bipolar II, rather than separately or under depressive disorders. This placement signals that the treatment philosophy should be aligned with bipolar management rather than with unipolar depression management. That alignment has practical consequences for medication decisions, covered in Chapter 8.

The Classification Debate

The case against positioning cyclothymia primarily within the bipolar spectrum rests on several arguments.

The first is empirical: the research base for cyclothymia as a biologically distinct entity, rather than simply a quantitatively milder version of bipolar disorders, is limited. Much of what is known about cyclothymia derives from studies designed around bipolar I and II, with cyclothymia included as a subgroup or extrapolated from closely related conditions. There are relatively few large clinical trials specifically designed for cyclothymia (Perugi et al., 2017a).

The second argument involves phenomenology. Critics of the bipolar spectrum model note that the cycling in cyclothymia looks different from the episodic cycling in bipolar I and II. The cycles are shorter, more rapid, more continuous, and more reactive to environmental triggers. Some researchers have argued that cyclothymia is better understood as a temperamental configuration, a biologically grounded but stable personality variant, rather than as an episodic mood disorder. This position is reflected in the historical tendency to classify cyclothymia under personality disorders in earlier classification systems.

The third argument is about classification utility. Placing cyclothymia within the bipolar spectrum can lead to overtreatment with heavy pharmacological approaches designed for more severe presentations. It can also lead to the social stigma associated with the bipolar label in populations where that stigma carries significant weight.

Position A: Cyclothymia Belongs on the Bipolar Spectrum

The evidence supporting the spectrum classification is substantial. The familial clustering of cyclothymia with bipolar I and bipolar II is well-documented: first-degree relatives of people with cyclothymia show elevated rates of bipolar disorder, and vice versa (Akiskal et al., 1977). This shared genetic architecture suggests biological continuity rather than categorical separation.

The progression data supports the spectrum position powerfully. Estimates consistently place the rate of progression from cyclothymia to bipolar I or bipolar II at between 15 and 50 percent (Perugi et al., 2017a). That range is wide and reflects genuine variability in study methodology, but no estimate approaches zero. Cyclothymia, left untreated, can progress. This trajectory is consistent with the spectrum model and inconsistent with a purely temperamental view.

The treatment response data also supports spectrum placement. Mood stabilizers, the foundation of bipolar treatment, show evidence of efficacy in cyclothymia at moderate doses. Antidepressants, which are first-line for unipolar depression, carry documented risks in cyclothymia of cycle-worsening and destabilization (covered in Chapter 8). A treatment profile that aligns with bipolar management is consistent with spectrum placement.

Position B: The Bipolar Frame Needs Qualifying

The case for qualifying the bipolar framing is not that cyclothymia is not a real condition; the evidence that it is a genuine mood disorder with functional consequences is clear. The case is that the bipolar label, applied uncritically, can mislead in specific ways.

The most important qualification concerns the nature of the cycling. Bipolar I and II episodes are typically weeks to months in length, with genuine periods of normal functioning between them. Cyclothymia's cycling is faster, more continuous, and more environmentally reactive. This difference in cycling pattern means that some therapeutic approaches designed for the episodic bipolar I or II picture, particularly approaches that focus on identifying and managing distinct episodes, translate imperfectly to cyclothymia.

The second qualification involves medication dosing philosophy. The "go slow and stay low" principle that Perugi and colleagues (2017b) apply to cyclothymia pharmacotherapy reflects the condition's particular sensitivity to medication effects: cyclothymia patients tend to be more sensitive to both the benefits and the side effects of mood-active medications than bipolar I patients. This sensitivity warrants a more conservative pharmacological approach than the bipolar label in isolation might suggest.

What the Debate Means for You

The practical upshot of this debate for the reader with cyclothymia is straightforward. The bipolar spectrum classification tells you that the treatment principles for your condition align with bipolar management rather than with pure depression management. It tells you that antidepressant monotherapy is likely to be insufficient and possibly counterproductive. It tells you that mood stabilization, circadian regularity, and psychotherapy designed for bipolar-spectrum presentations are the relevant evidence base.

It does not mean that you have bipolar disorder in the sense that people mean when they use that phrase in everyday conversation. It does not mean that your experience is the same as someone with bipolar I. It does not mean that you are at the severe end of any scale. You are at the lower-threshold end of a spectrum, which means that the spectrum's biology applies to your condition, and therefore its treatment principles apply, but the severity, duration, and intensity of your individual episodes are genuinely different.

Cases: Fallon and Garnet (Braided)

Both are composite illustrations.

Fallon, 29, had been managing a diagnosis of bipolar II for three years. The diagnostic picture was clear: two full hypomanic episodes, each lasting more than four consecutive days, during which family members independently noted that Fallon "wasn't themselves," combined with two major depressive episodes meeting full DSM-5 criteria for symptom number and duration. Fallon was on quetiapine and maintained relative stability with twice-yearly mood dips.

Garnet, 31, carried a recent cyclothymia diagnosis. Garnet's elevated periods lasted two to four days and produced recognizable but sub-threshold changes: somewhat reduced sleep, somewhat increased talkativeness, somewhat elevated self-confidence. Garnet's depressive periods lasted a similar duration, with anhedonia and fatigue as the dominant features. The pattern had repeated without a break exceeding six weeks for four years. Garnet reported that the bipolar II frame, which an earlier clinician had used tentatively, never quite fit: the episodes were not dramatic enough, not distinct enough from the background noise of daily mood variation.

Both Fallon and Garnet are on the bipolar spectrum. Both face progression risk if untreated. Their treatment approaches share a philosophical foundation: mood stabilization as the primary goal, attention to sleep and circadian regularity, caution with antidepressants. The clinical differences in their presentations reflect the spectrum in action: the same underlying biology producing different episode structure, different degrees of behavioral disruption, and different but related diagnostic outcomes.

The Honest Summary

What is settled: cyclothymia shares biological and familial features with the bipolar spectrum, responds to mood stabilization approaches rather than to pure antidepressant approaches, and carries a real risk of progression if untreated. The spectrum classification is the most clinically useful framing available and should guide treatment decisions.

What remains contested: whether cyclothymia is categorically a bipolar disorder in the phenomenological sense, whether the spectrum model fully captures its distinct rapid-cycling character, and how aggressively it should be pharmacologically managed. These questions remain open in the research literature. Sitting with that uncertainty, and making practical treatment decisions that reflect the best available evidence, is the honest position for both clinician and reader.

Chapter 5: Why Your Brain Cycles

Consider the last time you felt genuinely good without a reason for it. Not pleased about something specific, not relieved, not energized by coffee: just better than usual, more capable, lighter. You probably attributed it to something: a good night's sleep, a successful day, a piece of good news. The attribution felt correct. It probably was not entirely wrong. But for a brain with cyclothymia, the direction of causality runs differently than it does for most people. The brain doesn't improve in response to good circumstances. The circumstances look good because the brain has temporarily improved.

That distinction, between mood as a response to life and mood as a biological state that colors the interpretation of life, is central to understanding why cyclothymia happens and what can be done about it.

The Genetic Foundation

The most consistent biological finding in cyclothymia research is the role of genetic inheritance. First-degree relatives of people with bipolar I disorder show elevated rates of cyclothymia, and first-degree relatives of people with cyclothymia show elevated rates of both cyclothymia and bipolar spectrum presentations more broadly (Akiskal et al., 1977). This familial clustering is stronger than chance and suggests that the bipolar spectrum, including cyclothymia, has a genetic substrate.

The specific genes involved are not fully characterized. Cyclothymia does not have a single identified genetic cause. What the genetic data suggests is a **polygenic risk architecture**: multiple genes, each contributing a small increment to overall vulnerability, which interact with developmental history and environmental stress to produce the clinical presentation. This is similar to the genetic structure of bipolar I and II, which are also polygenic rather than Mendelian.

What this means practically is that having cyclothymia does not mean having a "broken" gene. It means having a genetic background that made your brain more likely to develop this particular pattern of mood regulation. It also means that the condition can be inherited, and that family members may be at elevated risk for mood disorders of their own.

Neurochemistry and Mood Cycling

The neurochemical basis of cyclothymia is incompletely understood, but research points to dysregulation in the same systems implicated in the broader bipolar spectrum: serotonergic pathways, dopaminergic pathways, and glutamatergic transmission. These systems are not simply "too high" or "too low" in the way that older models of depression proposed. They are dysregulated, meaning their activity is poorly calibrated to environmental demands and shifts in ways that are not proportional to external circumstances.

Serotonin is involved in mood regulation, sleep, and stress response. Serotonergic dysregulation contributes to the depressive component of cyclothymia and to the emotional reactivity and interpersonal sensitivity that characterize the cyclothymic temperament.

Dopamine is central to motivation, reward processing, and goal-directed behavior. The elevated energy, increased motivation, and pleasure in activity during hypomanic-like phases reflect dopaminergic activation. The anhedonia and motivational flatness of the depressive phase reflect its reduction.

Glutamate, the brain's primary excitatory neurotransmitter, has been increasingly implicated in mood disorders. Lamotrigine, one of the most commonly used medications in cyclothymia management, modulates glutamatergic activity, which may partially explain its efficacy.

Understanding the neurochemistry of cyclothymia does not require a biochemistry degree. The clinical takeaway is that the mood cycling reflects genuine biological state changes in the brain, not choices or character, and that medications capable of modulating these systems can meaningfully reduce the amplitude and frequency of the cycling.

The Circadian Clock Hypothesis

One of the most important insights in mood disorder research over the past four decades is the role of circadian rhythms in mood regulation. **Circadian rhythms** are the body's internal clock system, a collection of biological processes that run on approximately a 24-hour cycle and regulate sleep, hormone secretion, body temperature, alertness, and many other functions.

In a well-regulated circadian system, these cycles are synchronized internally with each other and anchored externally to environmental time cues, primarily light and social activity. When the circadian system is disrupted, through irregular sleep, shift work, jet lag, excessive light exposure at night, or major schedule changes, mood in vulnerable individuals can destabilize rapidly.

People with cyclothymia appear to have a less robust circadian system than average. Their internal clocks are more easily perturbed by external disruptions and less efficient at resynchronizing after disruption (Scott et al., 2022). This circadian vulnerability is one reason why sleep and routine have such outsized importance in cyclothymia management: they are not lifestyle preferences but compensatory mechanisms for a biological system that runs less stably than average.

The **social zeitgeber theory**, proposed by Ehlers, Frank, and Kupfer (1988), builds directly on this circadian vulnerability. It proposes that social time cues, the regular activities of daily life like mealtimes, social contact, and work, serve as external synchronizers (zeitgebers, from the German for "time givers") that anchor the biological clock. When those cues are disrupted, in someone with bipolar-spectrum vulnerability, the circadian system loses its anchoring and mood can shift accordingly. Chapter 6 covers the practical application of this theory through social rhythm therapy.

Triggers That Start a Cycle

Not all triggers for cyclothymia episodes are equal. Research consistently identifies a relatively small set of precipitants that carry the greatest risk.

Sleep disruption is the most consistent and powerful trigger across the bipolar spectrum. Even a single night of significantly reduced sleep can initiate an elevated phase in vulnerable individuals. The direction of causality is bidirectional: sleep disruption can trigger a hypomanic-like phase, and hypomanic-like phases reduce the perceived need for sleep, which further disrupts sleep and can sustain or amplify the episode. Chapter 7 addresses this relationship in detail.

Stress, particularly chronic moderate stress, is a well-documented precipitant. The stress does not need to be catastrophic to trigger a cycle. Sustained work pressure, relationship conflict, financial strain, or even positive but demanding life events (a promotion, a move, a major creative project) can push the system into a phase shift.

Substance use increases episode risk, particularly alcohol, cannabis, and stimulants. Alcohol is sedating in the short term but disrupts sleep architecture and is a depressant in the medium term. Cannabis can trigger elevated states in some people with cyclothymia and worsen depressive states in others. Stimulants, including prescription stimulants for ADHD, can precipitate hypomanic-like episodes in bipolar-spectrum presentations.

Major life events, even positive ones, carry risk through their disruption of routine and sleep. Travel across time zones (jet lag), childbirth, job changes, bereavement, and significant relationship transitions have all been documented as episode precipitants in cyclothymia.

Antidepressant medication without mood stabilization is a treatment-related trigger discussed in detail in Chapter 8. It deserves mention here because many readers will have experienced it: a period of antidepressant treatment that seemed to increase mood instability, cause agitation or accelerated thinking, or trigger a period of elevated mood that gave way to a more pronounced crash.

The Kindling Effect

The **kindling hypothesis**, developed by Post (1992) and applied to bipolar-spectrum disorders, proposes that each untreated mood episode lowers the threshold for the next one. The term comes from fire-starting: small pieces of kindling catch a spark more readily than larger logs, and each successful ignition makes the next one easier.

Applied to cyclothymia, the kindling model suggests that episodes which go untreated, or which are treated only partially, progressively sensitize the cycling system. Early episodes may require significant environmental stress to trigger. Later episodes may be triggered by progressively smaller disruptions, and eventually may occur without any identifiable external precipitant. This trajectory is not inevitable, and treatment substantially modifies it. But it is one of the strongest arguments for taking cyclothymia seriously and pursuing active management from the point of diagnosis.

Case 1: Hollis

A composite narrative.

Hollis had been fine through university. Not perfectly stable, not undisturbed, but functional. There were weeks of energy and weeks of difficulty, but nothing that disrupted the framework of a structured academic year with term dates, exam periods, and social rhythms built in.

The change came in the year after graduation. Hollis moved to a new city for a job that required irregular hours, frequently changing shift patterns, and evening work that pushed dinner and sleep times forward by three hours. Within four months, Hollis was cycling in a way that felt qualitatively different from anything before: elevated periods that arrived suddenly, lasted less than a week, and gave way to depressive periods that were longer and more impairing than anything Hollis had experienced. A GP visit attributed the low periods to adjustment difficulties and offered a short course of an antidepressant. The antidepressant increased the frequency of mood shifts. Three months later, Hollis was assessed by a psychiatrist who identified cyclothymia and pointed directly at the shift work pattern as the environmental trigger for the new severity.

What the case illustrates is the role of circadian disruption as an amplifier of an existing vulnerability. Hollis likely had cyclothymic biology across the university years, held in relative check by the external structure of academic life. Removing that structure while simultaneously imposing a chronobiologically disruptive work pattern was the combination that pushed a manageable underlying condition into a clinically significant one.

Case 2: Indigo

A composite labeled case.

Background: Indigo, a 22-year-old, was referred following an initial assessment for mood instability. Their mother had been diagnosed with bipolar II at age 38. Their maternal grandmother had been described, in family accounts, as someone who "ran hot and cold her whole life" and who had several hospitalizations for mood crises that went undocumented diagnostically.

Presentation: Indigo described a mood pattern that they had experienced, as far back as they could remember, as "always moving." High periods, during which they were sociable, creative, and impulsive, lasting three to five days. Low periods, during which they were withdrawn and unable to enjoy anything, lasting a similar duration. No period of stable mood exceeding three weeks in the past year.

Analysis: Family history consistent with bipolar-spectrum genetic loading across two generations. Clinical presentation meeting DSM-5-TR criteria for cyclothymia. Onset appeared in mid-adolescence but had not presented clinically until the current assessment.

Intervention: Psychoeducation provided first, followed by mood tracking and IPSRT referral. Medication discussion deferred pending mood data collection over eight weeks.

Teaching Points:

- Positive family history for bipolar-spectrum conditions substantially increases cyclothymia risk.
- Early onset (adolescence) is typical and means the condition has often been present long before clinical contact.
- A deferred medication decision pending solid mood data reflects good clinical practice for cyclothymia.

Pulling the Threads

The biology of cyclothymia is not fully mapped, and perhaps it never will be, given the complexity of the systems involved. But enough is understood to make a few things clear. The cycling is not a choice. It has genetic roots, neurochemical expression, circadian underpinnings, and environmental triggers that interact across time in predictable enough ways to be managed.

The question that now presents itself, and that the next several chapters address directly, is this: given that your brain cycles in this way, and given that you understand more precisely why it does so, what can you actually do about it?

Chapter 6: Social Rhythm Therapy

The plate that Joss's grandmother put on the table every evening at six-thirty was not remarkable. It held whatever had been cooked. It sat on the same oil-cloth that had been there for decades. Dinner happened at six-thirty because dinner had always happened at six-thirty. The time was not negotiated or reconsidered. It simply was.

Joss did not understand, during the years of living in that house, that the six-thirty plate was doing something to the brain. That the regularity of it, the predictability of that signal arriving at that hour, was one of the mechanisms by which a biological system with cyclothymic vulnerability had managed to function with relative stability into late middle age. Joss did not understand this until the plate was gone, the grandmother was gone, and the cycling, which had always been there at a low level, became something different.

Social zeitgebers are external time cues that synchronize the body's internal biological clock. The word comes from German: "zeit" meaning time, "geber" meaning giver. Mealtimes are zeitgebers. Consistent social contact is a zeitgeber. A regular work start time is a zeitgeber. Sleep onset at a consistent hour is a zeitgeber. These cues anchor the brain's circadian rhythm to the social world, helping to keep biological processes running on schedule. When the cues disappear or become irregular, the circadian system in a person with bipolar-spectrum vulnerability can lose its anchoring, and mood instability follows.

Social rhythm therapy is the clinical approach built on this understanding. It is, in the view of the available evidence, one of the most powerful non-pharmacological tools available for cyclothymia management. And it is, by a significant margin, the most under-explained concept in consumer mental health publishing.

What Social Zeitgebers Are

The social zeitgeber theory was proposed by Ehlers, Frank, and Kupfer in 1988, drawing on the biological finding that bipolar-spectrum disorders involve circadian rhythm dysregulation alongside mood instability. The theory made a specific and testable claim: that disruptions to the social cues that normally synchronize the circadian system are a key pathway through which stress triggers mood episodes in vulnerable individuals.

The stressor, on this model, does not directly cause the episode. Instead, the stressor disrupts the person's regular social rhythms, mealtimes shift, sleep times shift, social contact patterns change, routine evaporates. The disrupted social rhythms fail to provide the normal zeitgeber input to the biological clock. The clock loses its external anchoring. Circadian dysregulation follows, and in a person with bipolar-spectrum vulnerability, circadian dysregulation translates into mood instability (Ehlers et al., 1988).

This model explains several things that otherwise remain puzzling. It explains why stressors of very different types, a divorce, a promotion, a bereavement, a holiday, can all trigger mood episodes in someone with cyclothymia: they all share the feature of disrupting routine. It explains why even positive life events carry episode risk. It explains why mood often stabilizes when routine is re-established, even before any medication change. And it explains why sleep protection and routine maintenance are not merely lifestyle advice but genuinely therapeutic.

The Theory Behind the Practice

Interpersonal and Social Rhythm Therapy, usually abbreviated to **IPSRT**, is the structured psychotherapeutic intervention developed by Frank and colleagues to apply the social zeitgeber theory to clinical practice (Frank et al., 2000). It combines the social rhythm component, tracking and stabilizing daily routine, with an interpersonal component that addresses the relationship context in which rhythm disruptions typically occur.

In the original IPSRT trials with bipolar I patients, patients who received IPSRT had longer intervals before relapse and better overall outcomes than those who received clinical management alone (Frank et al., 2005). The effects were especially pronounced for the social rhythm component: patients who stabilized their social rhythms earlier in treatment had better outcomes than those who did not, regardless of other treatment factors.

The application of IPSRT to cyclothymia specifically is supported by the social zeitgeber theory, by the documented circadian vulnerability in cyclothymia, and by clinical practice. A 2004 case study by Ree and Harvey demonstrated measurable reductions in mood variability in a cyclothymia patient through a CBT intervention that emphasized routine and sleep stabilization. The evidence base for IPSRT in cyclothymia per se is less extensive than for bipolar I, but the theoretical rationale is strong and the clinical uptake in specialist mood disorder services has been consistent.

The Five Anchor Activities

The practical heart of social rhythm therapy is the concept of **anchor activities**. These are the daily activities whose timing matters most for circadian stability. Stabilizing the timing of these five activities is the minimum meaningful social rhythm intervention.

Wake time is the single most important anchor. The time you wake up in the morning is the primary "zeitgeber" for the entire circadian system. It sets the tone for when alertness peaks, when melatonin is released in the evening, and when sleep drive accumulates across the day. A consistent wake time, even if achieved imperfectly, is more stabilizing than almost any other single behavioral intervention in cyclothymia management.

The key principle is that wake time should be consistent even when sleep onset was late. If you went to bed at two in the morning, you still get up at seven, or at whatever your target time is. This is counterintuitive. It conflicts with the pull to "catch up on sleep" after a night of reduced or delayed sleep. But it is the evidence-supported approach, because a consistent wake time maintains the circadian anchor, while varying wake time in response to variable sleep onset allows the anchor to drift.

First social contact is the second anchor: the first substantive social interaction of the day, whether in person or by phone. This functions as a social cue that you are engaged in the world. For people who work from home or live alone, this may require deliberate design. A morning phone call with a friend, a scheduled conversation with a colleague, even walking to a coffee shop where there is a familiar face: these count as first social contact and carry zeitgeber value.

Start of daily activity or work is the third anchor. The time at which you begin the structured activity of your day serves as a social and cognitive cue. This does not require a rigid nine-to-five schedule. It requires a consistent start point.

Dinner time is the fourth anchor, and it is the one most people with irregular schedules most consistently fail to protect. Meal timing is a powerful biological signal: it synchronizes gut circadian rhythms, signals the transition from the active phase of the day to the recovery phase, and anchors the late-afternoon period that is often the most mood-vulnerable part of the day for people with cyclothymia. An irregular dinner time, eaten anywhere between five and nine depending on the day, provides a weak zeitgeber signal. A consistent dinner window provides a strong one.

Sleep onset time is the fifth anchor. This is less strictly controllable than wake time, since sleep onset depends on sleep drive, light exposure, and a number of other factors, but having a consistent target bedtime and protecting the pre-sleep routine that leads to it is the practical goal.

The power of anchor activity timing is not in any one of these activities individually. It is in the combined regularity they create: a daily schedule that repeats with enough consistency to provide reliable zeitgeber input to a circadian system that needs that input more than most.

Why Irregularity Is Dangerous

The risk of schedule irregularity in cyclothymia is not trivial, and it is worth being direct about why.

When social rhythms are disrupted, the circadian clock loses its external anchoring. In a person without bipolar-spectrum vulnerability, the clock will resynchronize relatively quickly once normal routine resumes. In a person with cyclothymia, the resynchronization is slower and less robust. The circadian dysregulation can persist for days after the precipitating disruption has ended, and during that dysregulated window, mood instability risk is elevated.

This means that schedule disruptions which other people navigate without significant consequence (a late night, a weekend of irregular eating and sleeping, a busy stretch at work that pushes everything later) carry disproportionate risk for the person with cyclothymia. It also means that the advice to "just relax and not worry so much about routine," while well-intentioned, is precisely backwards. The routine is not an anxiety management technique. It is a biological one.

None of this requires a joyless life of identical days. The goal is anchor stability, not total rigidity. You can travel. You can have late nights. You can have irregular workloads. The skill is in building re-anchoring strategies: when disruption occurs, moving back to the anchor routine as quickly as possible, rather than letting the disrupted schedule persist.

Building Your Social Rhythm

The practical starting point for social rhythm therapy is a **Social Rhythm Metric**: a daily log of the five anchor activities with their actual times, compared to your target times. The original Social Rhythm Metric used in IPSRT research includes more activities than the five described here, but for self-directed application, the five anchors are the minimum viable intervention.

Tracking your current anchor times for two weeks before making any changes is useful: it reveals the actual pattern of your schedule, which may differ from what you believe your schedule to be. Many people discovering their anchor patterns for the first time find more variability than they expected. A dinner time that they thought of as "around seven" turns out to range between five-thirty and nine-fifteen across the week. A wake time believed to be consistent varies by two and a half hours between weekdays and weekends.

Once the baseline is established, the goal is to narrow the range on each anchor, not to a single rigid time, but to a window. A target wake time of seven o'clock, with an acceptable range of six-thirty to seven-thirty, is a more achievable starting point than an absolute commitment to seven o'clock every day. Narrowing the window over time, and maintaining it across disruptions, is the skill being developed.

When disruptions do occur, the social rhythm metric serves as a return-to-baseline tool. After a holiday, a late night, a stressful week that pushed everything off schedule, the metric provides the specific targets to return to, preventing the disrupted schedule from becoming the new irregular normal.

When Rhythm Gets Disrupted

Social rhythm disruptions fall into two categories: planned and unplanned. Both require management, but the approaches differ.

For planned disruptions, the principle of protective advance scheduling applies. If you know that a work deadline next week will push your sleep time later for five consecutive nights, you can build in a partial mitigation: hold the morning anchor (wake time) as close to target as possible even with the late nights, maintain the dinner window, and plan a recovery period for the weekend after the deadline, not to sleep in but to protect the anchor times carefully through the re-anchoring period.

For unplanned disruptions, such as illness, unexpected demands, social events that run late, or emotional events that disrupt sleep, the goal is rapid return to anchor times rather than extended recovery. The evidence from circadian biology is that a prompt return to regular anchor times after disruption is more effective at resynchronizing the clock than extending the disrupted schedule in an attempt to recover.

The most common mistake people make after a disrupted period is allowing themselves a prolonged recovery that varies significantly from their usual schedule. The intention is to rest and recover. The circadian consequence is an extended period of anchor drift that can sustain the mood instability triggered by the original disruption. Counterintuitive as it feels, getting back to anchor times quickly, including the anchor wake time, tends to shorten the recovery period rather than extend it.

Case 1: Joss (Worked Example)

A composite worked example.

Joss, 38, had been diagnosed with cyclothymia six months earlier following assessment that confirmed a pattern dating to the late twenties. The immediate precipitating event for seeking assessment was a depressive phase so impairing that Joss had been unable to work for three weeks. The elevated phase before it had been the longest and most intense on record.

Step 1: Establishing the baseline. Joss began tracking anchor times on a daily log. Over two weeks, the data showed:

- Wake time: ranged from 6:15 a.m. on workdays to 10:00 a.m. on weekends. Saturday and Sunday sleep-ins were habitual.

- First social contact: highly variable. Some mornings no meaningful social contact occurred before noon.

- Work start: consistent on contract days (8:30 a.m.) but absent on freelance days, which could begin anywhere from 9:00 a.m. to 2:00 p.m.

- Dinner time: ranged from 6:00 to 9:30 p.m.

- Sleep onset target: no consistent target. Joss reported "going to bed when tired," which varied between 10:30 p.m. and 1:30 a.m.

Step 2: Identifying the highest-risk variable. The weekend wake time drift of nearly four hours was flagged as the primary target. A four-hour shift in wake time across the weekend represents a self-imposed jet lag equivalent, documented in the chronobiology literature as "social jet lag," and is associated with elevated mood instability risk (Scott et al., 2022).

Step 3: Setting the first anchor target. Joss set a wake time target of 7:00 a.m. with an acceptable range of 6:30 to 7:30, including weekends. This was the only anchor change for the first four weeks. Everything else was tracked but not yet modified.

Step 4: Outcome at four weeks. Joss's mood chart across the four weeks showed a reduction in peak-to-trough variability compared to the four weeks before the intervention. The elevated period that had been expected around week three based on the previous cycle pattern arrived, but at a lower peak rating (6.5 instead of 8) and resolved more quickly (five days instead of eleven). Joss attributed this tentatively to the weekend wake time change but noted it was too early to be certain.

Step 5: Adding the second anchor. At week five, a consistent dinner target of 7:00 p.m. (range 6:30 to 7:30) was added. Tracking continued.

The lesson from Joss's case is not that social rhythm therapy produces rapid, dramatic results. It is that small, consistent anchor changes can produce measurable mood stabilization within weeks, and that beginning with one anchor, protected consistently, is more effective than attempting to regularize the entire schedule simultaneously.

Case 2: Kestrel

A composite narrative.

Kestrel was a photographer whose work required travel, irregular shooting schedules, and frequent late events. The cyclothymia diagnosis had felt, initially, like a sentence: how could someone with their schedule possibly maintain the kind of routine that the IPSRT therapist described?

The answer, worked out over several months, was that the routine did not need to be externally visible. Kestrel could not control what time a wedding reception ended, or what time zone a destination assignment put them in. What Kestrel could control was the rapid return.

The practice that emerged was simple: for every disrupted anchor period, a return window. After a late event, the morning wake time held within thirty minutes of target. After a trip across time zones, two days of anchor protection before accepting any new work commitments. Dinner was eaten within the target window when in the home city; when traveling, a meal at the hotel at the local equivalent of the usual dinner hour substituted.

Over eight months of this practice, Kestrel tracked the cycling pattern on a daily chart. The elevated phases became shorter. The depressive phases, which had been the most impairing, became less severe and resolved more quickly. The cycling did not stop. It became, in Kestrel's word, narrower.

The practical lesson: social rhythm therapy is not an instruction to live an identical life every day. It is a framework for protecting a set of biological time anchors against disruption, and for returning to them rapidly when disruption occurs. In a life with genuine irregularity, the practice is about the return, not the absence of variation.

From Theory to Practice

Social rhythm therapy is the practitioner's answer to a specific biological problem: a circadian system that is less robust than average, more easily perturbed, and slower to resynchronize. The tool is not medication. It is time. Consistent, repeating, biological-clock-anchoring time.

For readers who are starting from scratch, the single most useful action is this: choose a wake time. Hold it for four weeks, including weekends. Track your mood twice daily. Review the chart at the end of the four weeks. That data, collected on the foundation of one protected anchor, is the beginning of a social rhythm practice.

The social rhythm is not separate from treatment. For cyclothymia, it is treatment. Chapter 7 turns to the most important single anchor: sleep.

Chapter 7: Sleep and Circadian Rhythms

In a large population study of people with bipolar-spectrum disorders, researchers found that sleep disturbance was present in more than 70 percent of participants even during periods of mood stability (Harvey et al., 2009). Not during episodes. Between them. The sleep problem was not a byproduct of the mood disorder. It was a co-traveling companion.

That figure changed something in how sleep is understood in the context of cyclothymia. Sleep disruption had been recognized for decades as a symptom of mood episodes: you don't sleep when you are hypomanic, you sleep too much when you are depressed. What the research clarified is that the disruption is structural, not merely symptomatic. The relationship between sleep and mood in cyclothymia is bidirectional, persistent, and more central than it first appears.

The Problem That Kept Being Missed

For most of the history of mood disorder treatment, sleep was treated as a consequence of mood. Treat the mood disorder successfully, and the sleep would follow. This is partly true. Effective mood stabilization does typically improve sleep. But it is not the whole picture.

The research on circadian rhythms and bipolar-spectrum disorders has demonstrated that circadian dysregulation, the misalignment of biological clock activity with the social and environmental day, is present during euthymia (stable mood) and not only during episodes (Scott et al., 2022). This means the sleep architecture is altered at a baseline level in people with cyclothymia, not only when they are in a mood episode. Treating mood without addressing the underlying circadian disruption leaves part of the pathology unaddressed.

The clinical implication is that sleep protection is not simply a coping strategy for feeling better. It is a direct intervention in one of the biological pathways through which cyclothymia produces mood instability.

Sleep Disruption as Trigger and Consequence

The relationship between sleep and mood episodes in cyclothymia runs in both directions, and understanding the bidirectionality is important for managing it.

Sleep disruption can trigger an elevated phase. This is one of the most robust findings in the bipolar-spectrum literature. Even a single night of significantly reduced sleep can initiate an elevated phase in vulnerable individuals, apparently through the same circadian pathway described in the previous chapter: reduced sleep disrupts circadian anchoring, circadian dysregulation follows, and mood instability emerges from the dysregulation.

Conversely, the onset of an elevated phase reduces the perceived need for sleep. One of the defining features of hypomania is feeling rested and energized on fewer hours than usual. This reduction in sleep is not simply a behavioral choice; it reflects a genuine change in the biology of sleep pressure during the elevated phase. The consequence is that the hypomanic-like phase and the associated sleep reduction amplify each other: the mood state reduces sleep, and the reduced sleep sustains or extends the mood state.

The low phase reverses this pattern. Hypersomnia, sleeping more than usual, is common during cyclothymia's depressive phases and can be substantial: ten to twelve hours of sleep with persistent fatigue is not unusual. This is distinct from the restorative sleep of someone who is genuinely tired. It is a symptom of the depressive state and does not reliably improve with more time in bed.

Reduced Sleep Need During Hypomania

The reduced sleep need of the hypomanic-like phase deserves specific attention because it is the point at which most people make the mistake that extends the episode.

During an elevated phase, the reduced sleep feels like a feature rather than a warning sign. Four or five hours leaves a person with cyclothymia feeling genuinely capable and energized. The impulse, reasonable under normal circumstances, is to use the time. To stay up later because there is no perceived cost to doing so. To run on the energy rather than protect against its departure.

The clinical evidence suggests that protecting sleep during an elevated phase, specifically increasing sleep duration back toward baseline and protecting a consistent sleep onset time, is one of the most effective ways to limit the phase's intensity and duration. This is not comfortable advice. The elevated phase is the part of the cycle that many people with cyclothymia value, or at minimum prefer over the low. The instruction to go to bed earlier when you feel productive and capable conflicts with the biological pull of the phase. But the data on circadian stabilization, and the downstream consequence of a shorter, less intense elevated phase for the subsequent low, supports it.

A useful frame for this is the debt model of sleep in cyclothymia. Sleep debt accumulated during an elevated phase is paid back in the low phase, with interest. A five-night run of five-hour nights typically produces not just five nights of normal compensatory sleep but an extended depressive episode of greater severity. Protecting sleep during the elevated phase is, in part, protecting the low phase that follows.

Protecting Sleep as Treatment

Specific sleep protection strategies for cyclothymia go beyond the generic sleep hygiene advice that applies to the general population. The following are the approaches with the best evidence-to-rationale ratio for bipolar-spectrum presentations.

Light management is among the most powerful and least commonly used tools. Morning bright light exposure, within thirty to sixty minutes of waking, advances the circadian phase and strengthens the biological anchor. Evening light reduction, particularly the bluespectrum light emitted by screens, prevents the circadian system from receiving false "daytime" signals that delay sleep onset. The practical application is simple: some form of morning light within the first hour of waking (a walk outside is ideal but sitting near a window suffices), and reduced screen brightness after nine in the evening, or the use of blue-light filtering settings.

Stimulus control is the practice of using the bed only for sleep, removing from the bedroom the activities that train the brain to associate the bed with wakefulness: screens, work, eating. The bed signals sleep. That signal is weakened when the bed is used for everything. For someone with cyclothymia's circadian vulnerability, a strong sleep-bed association matters more than for the average person.

Pre-sleep routine is the consistent sequence of activities in the thirty to sixty minutes before sleep onset that signals to the circadian system that sleep is approaching. A bath or shower (the subsequent body temperature drop facilitates sleep onset), a period of reduced stimulation, consistent lighting, no new work or problem-solving. The content matters less than the consistency: the brain learns the signal through repetition.

Alcohol reduction is relevant here because of alcohol's specific effect on sleep architecture. While alcohol is sedating in the short term and may help the onset of sleep, it disrupts the second half of the night's sleep architecture, reducing REM sleep and increasing early-morning waking. For a brain with cyclothymia's sleep vulnerability, this is particularly costly, and the "good night's sleep" facilitated by alcohol is typically not restorative.

What to Do in the Low Phase

The depressive phase of cyclothymia presents a different sleep challenge. Hypersomnia, the pull to sleep much more than usual, is common and difficult to manage because it conflicts with the limited energy available to act on any protective strategy.

The evidence for low-phase sleep management in cyclothymia is thinner than for elevated phase sleep, but the social rhythm therapy framework offers a practical approach: maintain the anchor wake time even during the low phase, as closely as possible. Extended time in bed during the low phase does not accelerate recovery and may prolong it by reducing the sleep pressure that drives the eventual normalization of sleep onset. The discomfort of getting up at the usual time when the low phase makes every movement expensive is real and significant. It is still worth doing.

Activity scheduling, a tool from behavioral activation approaches, also helps during the low phase: planning small, achievable activities for the morning hours after the anchor wake time, creating a minimal but functioning daily structure that is easier to maintain than a completely unstructured recovery period.

Case 1: Linden

A composite labeled clinical case.

Background: Linden, a 40-year-old software developer, was referred following a third hypomanic-like episode in fourteen months, each of which had been followed by a depressive episode requiring sick leave. Mood tracking had confirmed the cyclothymia pattern. Mood stabilizer medication was under discussion but had not yet been started.

Presentation: Linden's mood chart showed a consistent pattern: the onset of elevated phases was preceded, by three to five days, by a reduction in sleep from a baseline of seven and a half hours to five or fewer. The sleep reduction was not experienced as insomnia. Linden reported feeling less need for sleep and typically used the additional hours productively, staying up later to complete work projects.

Analysis: The sleep reduction was identified as both a prodromal marker and a likely precipitant of the elevated phase. The bidirectional relationship was operational: reduced sleep was triggering and sustaining the elevated phases, and the elevated phases were reducing sleep pressure, extending the reduction.

Intervention: A sleep protection protocol was implemented as the first intervention ahead of medication. Linden was asked to set a target sleep window of 10:30 p.m. to 6:00 a.m. and to begin protecting the sleep onset time specifically when ratings exceeded 6.5 on the mood chart for more than two consecutive days. Blue-light reduction after 9:30 p.m. was implemented. Alcohol was reduced.

Outcome: Over the following six months, Linden recorded two mild elevated-phase periods that did not progress to the peak intensity of previous episodes. Both were preceded by the familiar sleep reduction, but the protection of the sleep onset time appeared to limit the phase's duration to five days rather than the previous ten to fourteen. Linden described the protocol as "annoying but undeniably working."

Teaching Points:

- Sleep reduction is often both a prodromal sign and an active precipitant of elevated phases in cyclothymia, not only a symptom.
- Non-pharmacological sleep protection can be introduced before or alongside medication and may meaningfully reduce episode intensity.
- Mood chart data is essential for identifying the sleep-mood pattern in individual cases.

Case 2: Merritt

A composite narrative.

Merritt had known about the sleep connection in a general way since the IPSRT sessions began, but it was the low phase that felt unmanageable, not the highs. The highs were disruptive, but they had a quality of aliveness that the lows entirely lacked. During the lows, ten hours of sleep left Merritt feeling no more rested than four. The pull to stay in bed was not laziness. It was absence.

The anchor wake time strategy was introduced as a two-week experiment. The target was 7:30 a.m., every day, regardless of when sleep had come the night before. Merritt did not believe it would help. Merritt also did not have an alternative strategy.

The first week was difficult: mornings arrived with a quality of pointlessness that made getting up feel theatrical. But the therapist had been specific about the goal: not feeling better immediately after rising, which was not realistic, but returning the circadian anchor to its usual position. The feeling would follow the physiology, not precede it.

By the end of the second week, Merritt noticed that the afternoon period, usually the most depleted point of the low phase, was marginally less severe. The pattern continued over four weeks, with the low phase resolving three days earlier than the previous episode's average. The elevated phase that followed was tracked carefully. It peaked at 7 on the mood chart rather than the previous 8.5. The subsequent low was the mildest in two years.

Merritt later described it as finding out that the thing you had been told to do was not the thing you wanted to do, and was also the thing that actually worked.

The Practitioner's Bottom Line

Three things are true of sleep in cyclothymia, and all three need to be held simultaneously.

Sleep disruption is a trigger, not just a symptom. Treating it as consequence rather than cause leaves the triggering pathway active.

Sleep protection during the elevated phase, specifically protecting sleep onset time and duration, is one of the most effective tools for limiting elevated phase intensity, even though it conflicts with the pull of the phase.

Anchor wake time maintenance during the low phase does not eliminate the low, but it limits the circadian drift that can extend and deepen the depressive period.

Sleep, managed well, does not cure cyclothymia. It narrows the cycling. And narrowing the cycling, consistently, across months and years, is how the condition becomes manageable.

Chapter 8: Medications and Cyclothymia

Here is what the research actually admits: there are no medications with specific FDA approval for cyclothymia. The pharmacological treatment of cyclothymia borrows from the bipolar I and II evidence base, applies it at lower doses with greater caution, and relies on clinical experience and expert consensus rather than large, dedicated cyclothymia-specific trials. The field knows considerably less about what works best in cyclothymia than it does about what works in bipolar I, and clinicians who present the medication question with false confidence are working beyond the evidence they have.

That honest admission is also, usefully, the beginning of genuine clarity. Because while the evidence base has gaps, it is not empty. The treatment principles that emerge from what is known are consistent and clinically meaningful. What follows is the clearest, most current account of those principles in plain language.

Why Medication Decisions Are Complicated

Cyclothymia presents specific pharmacological challenges that are worth naming before the individual options are described.

The first challenge is the condition's high medication sensitivity. Perugi and colleagues (2017b) describe cyclothymia as requiring a "go slow and stay low" approach to pharmacotherapy because people with cyclothymia tend to be more sensitive to mood-active medications than people with bipolar I. This sensitivity operates in both directions: response to small doses can be surprisingly good, and adverse effects, including medication-induced cycling, can appear at doses that would be unremarkable in a bipolar I patient.

The second challenge is the lack of dedicated trials. Most of what is known about mood stabilizer use in cyclothymia comes from extrapolation of bipolar I and II data, expert consensus statements, and case series rather than large randomized controlled trials. This is a genuine limitation of the evidence base, not a reason to avoid treatment. It is a reason to approach medication decisions in partnership with a prescriber, with documented mood tracking data, and with clear monitoring of response and adverse effects.

The third challenge is the bidirectional symptom profile. Cyclothymia involves both elevated and depressive states, and a medication that helps one may worsen the other or increase the frequency of switching between them. This is not hypothetical: antidepressants, the most commonly prescribed treatment for the depressive component, carry documented risks of destabilizing the cycling in bipolar-spectrum presentations. This is the most important piece of pharmacological information in this chapter.

The Antidepressant Problem

The antidepressant problem in cyclothymia is real, consistent in the clinical literature, and still widely underappreciated at the point of prescribing.

The clinical picture that leads to it is straightforward. A person with cyclothymia presents during a depressive phase. The depressive symptoms are genuine and impairing. The clinician, who may not have identified the cyclothymic pattern, prescribes an SSRI or SNRI. This is not a bad-faith decision: the presenting symptoms look like depression, and antidepressants are first-line for depression.

The problem arises because cyclothymia is not unipolar depression. It is a bipolar-spectrum condition, and bipolar-spectrum conditions respond differently to antidepressants than unipolar depression does. The specific risks, documented across the bipolar spectrum and explicitly described for cyclothymia by Perugi and colleagues (2017b), include increased cycling frequency (the mood switches between poles more often), amplified amplitude (the highs become higher and the lows become lower), induction of chronic mixed depressive states (a combination of depressive symptoms with activation and agitation that is among the hardest states to treat), and, in some individuals, acceleration of progression to full bipolar episodes.

The reason for these effects is not fully characterized, but the current understanding is that antidepressants activate mood without providing the stabilizing effect that mood stabilizers produce. In a cycling brain, activation without stabilization can push the system further into the cycling pattern rather than out of it.

This is not a categorical statement that antidepressants cannot be used in cyclothymia. A selected subgroup of cyclothymia patients do benefit from low-dose antidepressants, particularly when a specific anxious-depressive component is prominent and when they are used alongside a mood stabilizer (Perugi et al., 2017b). The clinical consensus, however, is that antidepressant monotherapy in cyclothymia is a poor first choice, and that the evidence for mood stabilizers as the first pharmacological intervention is stronger.

For readers who were prescribed antidepressants before receiving a cyclothymia diagnosis, and who noticed increased agitation, faster cycling, or a worsening of their mood instability on those medications, this chapter provides the clinical explanation for that experience. It is worth discussing with a prescriber.

Mood Stabilizers and the Evidence

Mood stabilizers are the pharmacological cornerstone of cyclothymia treatment. The term refers to a heterogeneous group of medications, including lithium and certain anticonvulsant medications, that reduce the amplitude and frequency of mood cycling across both poles.

The evidence for mood stabilizer use in cyclothymia specifically comes primarily from open studies, case series, and expert consensus rather than large randomized trials. The consistent finding across these sources is mild to moderate efficacy for reducing depressive episodes and for stabilizing the cycling pattern overall (Perugi et al., 2017b).

The absence of large dedicated trials is a gap in the evidence base, not evidence of inefficacy.

The choice between available mood stabilizers in cyclothymia is guided by the specific clinical picture: which symptoms predominate, what the comorbidity profile is, and what the person's individual response history suggests.

Lithium

Lithium is the oldest mood stabilizer in clinical use and the most extensively studied across the bipolar spectrum. It has demonstrated efficacy in preventing both manic and depressive episodes in bipolar I disorder, and the evidence for its use in cyclothymia, while less extensive, is consistent with a moderate stabilizing effect.

A particularly interesting finding in the cyclothymia literature is that people with a cyclothymic temperament may show a stronger response to lithium than people with other bipolar presentations (Perugi et al., 2017b). If this finding holds across larger samples, it would suggest that the cyclothymic biology may have specific pharmacological characteristics that are responsive to lithium's mechanism of action.

Lithium is the preferred option when the predominant clinical feature is marked affective intensity, strong mood cycling with clear elevated and depressive phases, and a family history consistent with bipolar spectrum. Its monitoring requirements, regular blood tests to check lithium levels and kidney and thyroid function, make it more demanding to maintain than some alternatives, but these requirements are manageable with a cooperative prescriber relationship.

The effective lithium dose in cyclothymia is typically at the lower end of the therapeutic range used in bipolar I. The "go slow and stay low" principle applies: starting doses are conservative, titration is slow, and the target serum level is generally lower than in bipolar I management.

Valproate

Valproate (valproic acid, divalproex sodium) is an anticonvulsant medication with well-established efficacy as a mood stabilizer in bipolar I disorder. In cyclothymia, it is the preferred option when anxiety is a prominent feature of the clinical picture, when mixed states (simultaneous presence of depressive and elevated symptoms) predominate, or when the elevated phases are characterized more by irritability than by euphoric elevation (Perugi et al., 2017b).

Jacobsen (1993) reported benefit from low-dose valproate specifically in cyclothymia and mild rapid cycling disorder in an early clinical series, and the clinical consensus has held this position. The relevant doses in cyclothymia tend to be lower than in bipolar I, consistent with the high medication sensitivity profile of the condition.

Valproate carries important safety considerations, particularly for women of childbearing potential. It carries a documented risk of neural tube defects in fetal development and has been associated with lower IQ scores in children exposed in utero. Current guidelines in many countries, including the UK's Medicines and Healthcare products Regulatory Agency (MHRA), recommend against valproate use in women of reproductive age unless there is no viable alternative and a pregnancy prevention program is in place. Any woman considering valproate should have a thorough discussion with their prescriber about this risk before starting treatment.

Lamotrigine

Lamotrigine is an anticonvulsant medication with a profile particularly suited to bipolar-spectrum presentations dominated by the depressive pole. It has demonstrated efficacy in preventing depressive episodes in bipolar II disorder, and its tolerability profile, characterized by fewer side effects than lithium or valproate at therapeutic doses, makes it one of the more commonly used first choices in cyclothymia when the depressive phase is the most impairing symptom.

The clinical consensus in cyclothymia is that lamotrigine is preferred when the anxious-depressive polarity is dominant: when the cycling is characterized more by depressive lows than by elevated highs, when anxiety accompanies the depressive phase, and when the person is particularly sensitive to medication side effects (Perugi et al., 2017b).

Lamotrigine requires slow dose titration because of the risk of a serious skin rash (Stevens-Johnson syndrome) if the dose is increased too rapidly. This is uncommon but severe, and it is the reason that lamotrigine prescribing follows a very specific dose escalation schedule. It is not a sign that the medication is dangerous at therapeutic doses; it is a reason to follow the prescribed titration schedule precisely.

An important finding from bipolar spectrum research is that combining lamotrigine with lithium can produce synergistic antidepressant effects beyond what either medication achieves alone. Some cyclothymia patients benefit from dual therapy, particularly when the depressive component is refractory to single-agent treatment (Perugi et al., 2017b).

Antipsychotics as Adjuncts

Atypical antipsychotic medications, including quetiapine, olanzapine, and aripiprazole, are sometimes used in cyclothymia as adjuncts to mood stabilizers rather than as primary treatments. They carry evidence for efficacy in bipolar depression and as mood-stabilizing agents across the spectrum, but their side effect profiles, including metabolic effects, weight gain, and sedation at therapeutic doses, make them less attractive as long-term first choices in a condition that may require decades of management.

When they are used in cyclothymia, it is typically for short periods to manage a specific episode or acute destabilization, rather than as maintenance treatment. The decision to use them should involve a specific discussion of the intended duration and the monitoring plan.

The High Medication Sensitivity Profile

Cyclothymia's high sensitivity to mood-active medications is worth restating because it has direct practical implications for how the medication experience is managed.

People with cyclothymia often notice medication effects at lower doses than expected, both therapeutic and adverse. This means that starting at the lower end of the prescribed dose range, and titrating slowly, is not timidity but good clinical practice. It also means that the absence of effect at very low doses is not necessarily an indication to abandon a medication: reaching the minimally effective dose may require patience.

It also means that changes in medication, including starting, stopping, or changing dose, carry higher risk of triggering mood instability than they would in the average patient. Medication changes should be made one at a time, with mood tracking in place around the change, and with the prescriber aware that you are monitoring for any phase shifts associated with the change.

The Medication Conversation

A productive medication conversation with a prescriber for cyclothymia should include several specific components that are not always covered in a standard psychiatric appointment.

Your medication history should be documented: specifically, what you have taken before, what the effect was, whether you noticed any change in the cycling frequency or amplitude during or after taking it, and what led to discontinuation if that applies.

Your current mood chart data should be brought to the appointment. A prescriber who can see two to three months of mood tracking data has a much clearer picture of the cycling pattern than one who relies on your retrospective description of how you have been "in general."

The question of polarity should be discussed: which pole is currently more impairing, the elevated phases or the depressive phases? The answer influences which medication is the better first choice.

The monitoring plan should be explicit: what is the target symptom, what would constitute a sufficient response, over what time frame, and what would indicate that the medication should be reconsidered.

Case 1: Nyx

A composite narrative.

Nyx's first SSRI was prescribed at 23, following what Nyx later identified as a depressive phase that had been relatively mild by previous standards. It helped, initially. The depression lifted. Nyx felt more energetic. More confident. A better version.

Within three weeks, the confidence had become something else. Nyx was making calls at midnight about a business idea, speaking too fast for colleagues to follow, cancelling commitments because something more urgent kept presenting itself. The feeling lasted nine days. What followed lasted three weeks and was the worst low Nyx had experienced.

The prescribing GP doubled the SSRI dose. The next cycle arrived within six weeks, shorter at the top and longer at the bottom. Nyx requested a referral to psychiatry.

The psychiatrist's assessment documented a two-year cycling pattern that had predated the antidepressant and had clearly worsened since its introduction. The SSRI was tapered and discontinued. Lamotrigine was started at 25mg, increased slowly across eight weeks to 100mg. Mood tracking showed a reduction in cycling frequency over the following four months. The elevated phases became shorter. The depressive phases, Nyx said, stopped feeling bottomless.

"It was like someone turned the volume down," Nyx reported at twelve months. "Not off. Down."

The case illustrates the antidepressant problem in clinical sequence: an SSRI appropriately prescribed for what appeared to be unipolar depression, worsening cycling in an underlying bipolar-spectrum condition, and the clinical shift required when the full diagnostic picture became available.

Cases: Oakley and Pax (Braided)

Both are composite illustrations.

Oakley, 44, presented with a cyclothymia diagnosis confirmed eighteen months earlier and a mood pattern in which the elevated phases were mild and brief but the depressive phases were significantly impairing, lasting two to three weeks and characterized by heavy anhedonia and social withdrawal. Anxiety was prominent throughout. Lamotrigine titrated to 150mg over twelve weeks produced a meaningful reduction in depressive phase frequency and severity. Oakley reported reduced anxiety as an additional benefit. Elevated phases were essentially unchanged but were already sub-threshold for impairment.

Pax, 37, had a mirror clinical picture: depressive phases were mild and brief, but elevated phases were impairing through their associated impulsivity and interpersonal consequences. Mixed states were common. Valproate at a low dose (500mg/day) produced a reduction in elevated phase intensity and fewer mixed episodes. Depressive phases were monitored but did not worsen.

Both Oakley and Pax were managed on mood stabilizers. The choice of agent was guided by polarity, not by the diagnosis label alone. The depressive-dominant picture pointed toward lamotrigine; the elevated and mixed-dominant picture pointed toward valproate. Neither was prescribed antidepressants as primary treatment.

What We Now Know

The pharmacological treatment of cyclothymia is incomplete in its evidence base, but its principles are clear. Mood stabilizers are the appropriate foundation. The choice between lithium, valproate, and lamotrigine is guided by the predominant polarity and the individual clinical picture. Antidepressants carry a documented risk of cycling destabilization and are not appropriate as first-line monotherapy for cyclothymia. Medication sensitivity is high and warrants slow titration and close monitoring.

Chapter 9 turns from pharmacological treatment to the psychological approaches that work alongside medication and, for some people, in its absence.

Chapter 9: Therapy That Works

Rumi came to IPSRT after four years of CBT that had been, in Rumi's own assessment, "useful but somehow beside the point." The CBT had helped with anxiety. It had provided cognitive tools for challenging catastrophic thinking during low phases. What it had not addressed was the cycling itself, the pattern of the mood rather than the content of the thoughts produced during each phase. Rumi still cycled. The cycling just had slightly better thinking wrapped around it.

Solstice came to the same therapy model from a different direction: a referral from a psychiatrist who had started Solstice on lamotrigine six months earlier and wanted to complement the pharmacological work with psychological support. Solstice had never done any psychotherapy before.

One year later, both Rumi and Solstice were in what their respective therapists described as a period of meaningful clinical improvement. Neither was in remission. Both were cycling less frequently and with lower amplitude. The similarity in outcome came from different therapeutic histories and different entry points into the same approach.

This is what the evidence looks like for psychological treatment in cyclothymia: not dramatic transformation in a single modality, but consistent, moderate, meaningful reduction in cycling frequency and severity from a small number of approaches that are specifically adapted to the bipolar-spectrum profile of the condition.

CBT Adapted for Cyclothymia

Standard cognitive behavioral therapy as originally developed for depression focuses on identifying and challenging negative automatic thoughts and the dysfunctional belief systems that generate them. This approach applies meaningfully to the depressive phase of cyclothymia. It applies much less well to the elevated phase, where the thoughts are not negative but are inflated and accelerated in ways that CBT's thought-challenging approach was not designed to address.

The adaptation of CBT for cyclothymia and related bipolar-spectrum presentations involves several key modifications.

The first modification is **circadian emphasis**: therapy sessions incorporate explicit attention to sleep, routine, and the circadian context of mood shifts. The CBT case described by Ree and Harvey (2004) involved a patient with cyclothymia who received a twenty-session CBT intervention with specific attention to sleep regularization and circadian rhythm stabilization. The intervention produced measurable reductions in daily mood variability and extended sleep across the treatment period.

The second modification is **phase-specific intervention**: different CBT tools are applied to different phases. Thought challenging and behavioral activation are appropriate for the depressive phase. During elevated phases, the relevant CBT targets are behavioral moderation (slowing down activity, protecting sleep, postponing major decisions), rather than thought challenging, since the elevated-phase thoughts are not characteristically negative.

The third modification is **mood monitoring as a cognitive tool**: regular, structured mood tracking is integrated into the CBT process as both a data source and a cognitive intervention. The act of recording mood twice daily builds metacognitive awareness of the cycling pattern, which is itself a therapeutic mechanism, separate from the specific CBT techniques applied.

Well-Being Therapy and the Fava Approach

Well-Being Therapy is a psychological intervention developed by Giovanni Fava and colleagues, based on Carol Ryff's model of psychological well-being. It focuses not on symptom reduction but on building the six domains of positive mental health: autonomy, environmental mastery, personal growth, positive relations with others, purpose in life, and self-acceptance.

The application of WBT to cyclothymia emerged from a clinical observation that standard depression-focused CBT addressed only one dimension of the cyclothymia picture. Fava and colleagues (2011) tested a sequential combination of standard CBT followed by Well-Being Therapy in a small sample of cyclothymia patients and reported significantly greater improvement compared to clinical management alone across two years of follow-up. Both clinical and well-being indicators improved, with particular effects on personal growth and positive relations.

The logic of the sequential approach is compelling. CBT reduces the distress associated with cyclothymia's depressive and elevated phases. Well-Being Therapy then builds the positive psychological resources that provide a buffer against the cycling, specifically the sense of purpose, autonomy, and positive connection that makes the stable periods more robust and reduces the pull of the elevated phase as the sole source of vitality and capability.

This combination is not yet standard practice across all clinical settings, but it is available and the evidence supports considering it, particularly for readers who have had good results from CBT for specific symptoms but find themselves returning to the same cycling pattern despite the cognitive gains.

Interpersonal and Social Rhythm Therapy in the Therapy Room

Chapter 6 introduced IPSRT as a framework for social rhythm self-management. In its full clinical form, IPSRT is a structured psychotherapy delivered over several months by a trained therapist, combining the social rhythm component with a focused interpersonal component.

The interpersonal component of IPSRT addresses four possible problem areas that are particularly relevant to cyclothymia: grief (including grief for the person's previous self-concept, before the diagnosis), role transitions (the life changes that precipitate mood episodes and that require adjustment), interpersonal disputes (the relationship conflicts generated by cycling mood), and interpersonal deficits (the social isolation and skill gaps that can develop over years of cycling without diagnosis).

In the clinical research, the interpersonal component added its own contribution to outcome beyond the social rhythm component alone. This makes clinical sense: the most common triggers for social rhythm disruption in real life are interpersonal events. A relationship ending disrupts sleep, meals, and social contact simultaneously. A conflict with a colleague makes the work schedule feel unbearable. Addressing both the schedule and the relational context of disruption produces better outcomes than addressing either alone.

If IPSRT is not available in your area, adaptations are possible. A therapist who is not formally trained in IPSRT but who is familiar with bipolar-spectrum presentations and who is willing to incorporate mood tracking and anchor time review into sessions can approximate the key elements. The social rhythm self-management framework described in Chapter 6 can also be applied without a therapist, though a therapeutic relationship adds monitoring, accountability, and the interpersonal work that the self-management approach cannot replicate.

DBT Skills as a Complement

Dialectical Behavior Therapy, developed by Marsha Linehan for borderline personality disorder, has been adapted for use across a range of presentations involving emotion dysregulation. It is not a primary evidence-based treatment for cyclothymia, but several of its skill modules are specifically relevant to the condition.

Emotion regulation skills include identifying and labeling emotional states, reducing vulnerability to emotional mind, and building positive experiences. These are directly useful for managing the phase transitions of cyclothymia, particularly the shift into the depressive state from the elevated phase.

Distress tolerance skills include crisis survival strategies for acute difficult moments and acceptance skills for situations that cannot be immediately changed. During the most impairing periods of a depressive phase, distress tolerance tools provide a way of surviving the state without making it worse.

Interpersonal effectiveness skills address communication and relationship maintenance in a way that is practically useful for the relational challenges created by cyclothymia cycling, covered in Chapter 10.

DBT in its full format is a substantial commitment and may be more appropriate as a primary treatment if a comorbid condition (such as BPD) is present alongside cyclothymia. As a skills supplement, selected DBT modules can be accessed through self-guided DBT workbooks or through brief skills groups without requiring full individual DBT therapy.

What to Look for in a Therapist

Finding a therapist who is well-suited to working with cyclothymia requires more specificity than many referral processes provide. The following criteria are useful guides.

Experience with mood disorders and bipolar-spectrum presentations is the most important criterion. A therapist who has worked primarily with anxiety disorders or personality disorders may have relevant skills, but their conceptual model of cyclothymia may not be current or accurate. Asking directly about their experience with bipolar-spectrum conditions, specifically cyclothymia if possible, is appropriate.

Familiarity with IPSRT, or at minimum with the social rhythm framework, is a significant asset. Not all therapists are trained in IPSRT, and that training is not available everywhere, but a therapist who understands the circadian framework and can incorporate mood tracking into sessions brings a specific competence that generic CBT does not.

Red Flags

A therapist who describes cyclothymia primarily as a personality issue, who dismisses the bipolar-spectrum framing, or who moves quickly to a BPD conceptualization without a thorough mood history assessment is working from an outdated or incomplete model. This is not necessarily a reason to abandon a therapeutic relationship that is otherwise productive, but it is worth a direct conversation about the diagnostic framework being used.

A therapist who does not ask about medication history, who does not ask about elevated phases, or who focuses exclusively on the depressive component without acknowledging the cycling is similarly missing a significant dimension of the clinical picture.

Therapy for cyclothymia cannot eliminate the cycling. A therapist who promises that it can is overpromising. The goal is reduction in cycling frequency and amplitude, better phase management, and improved quality of life within the context of the condition.

Case 1: Rumi (Worked Example)

A composite worked example illustrating the IPSRT process.

Rumi was referred to IPSRT after the CBT-without-circadian-focus had provided partial benefit. The first four sessions were assessment-focused: mapping the mood history, identifying the circadian pattern, and establishing the interpersonal context in which cycling disruptions typically occurred.

Session 1-4: Assessment. The mood chart established a cycling period of approximately eighteen days: nine days elevated, nine days depressed. The elevated phases were triggered consistently by one of three contexts: a significant creative project going well, a developing romantic interest, or a period of reduced sleep following a social event. The therapist noted that all three triggers shared the feature of social activation combined with schedule disruption.

Sessions 5-12: Social rhythm stabilization. Rumi and the therapist identified the five anchor activities and established target times for each. The wake time and dinner time were the most variable in the baseline data. A target wake time of 7:00 a.m. was set, with an acceptable range of 6:30 to 7:30. A dinner window of 7:00 to 8:00 p.m. was established. Mood tracking was reviewed weekly.

Sessions 13-20: Interpersonal work. The focus shifted to the interpersonal context of Rumi's cycling, particularly a pattern in which new relationships intensified during elevated phases and were damaged by the subsequent withdrawal. Role transition work addressed the grief associated with relationships that had ended before the cyclothymia diagnosis explained the pattern.

Outcome: At the end of twenty sessions, Rumi's mood chart showed a cycle length that had extended to approximately twenty-four days and a peak-to-trough amplitude that had narrowed by approximately 30 percent compared to the pre-treatment baseline. The most salient subjective change Rumi described was the ability to recognize a rising phase before it fully arrived and make different choices about sleep and social commitments.

"I still go up," Rumi said. "I just don't go as far up. And I've stopped being surprised when it ends."

Case 2: Solstice

A composite narrative.

Solstice had never been in therapy before the psychiatrist's referral. The skepticism was considerable. Sitting in a room talking about feelings seemed far removed from the problem of a brain that cycled in ways that had cost Solstice two relationships and one job over the previous four years.

The IPSRT therapist did not spend much time on feelings in the early sessions. Mostly, they looked at charts. At what time did Solstice wake up on Saturday versus Thursday? How many hours between the last meal and sleep onset? When did the mood rating last cross above 7, and what had happened to sleep in the preceding three days?

It was, Solstice noted, oddly scientific for something that was supposed to be therapy.

The interpersonal component arrived in month three, when the therapist began asking about the job that had been lost. Not the job exactly: what had happened in the weeks before the performance review that had gone badly. What the social contact pattern had looked like. What time dinner had been happening.

Solstice had been traveling for work for six consecutive weeks before the review. Time zones shifting every few days. Dinner when the client wanted dinner. Sleep when the schedule allowed it. The anchor had drifted so completely that by the review date, Solstice was on day eleven of a depressive phase that nobody in the room except Solstice knew about.

The retrospective analysis of the lost job through a circadian lens was, Solstice said later, more useful than anything else that had happened in therapy. Because it meant the same thing did not have to happen again.

Putting It to Work

What changed for Rumi over twenty sessions of IPSRT was not the cycling itself: Rumi was still cycling at the end of treatment. What changed was the relationship to the cycling. The phases became recognizable earlier. The behavioral responses to the early warning signs became practiced rather than improvised. The interpersonal damage of the elevated phase was reduced by building the capacity to recognize it before the most costly decisions were made.

That is not a cure. It is, for many people with cyclothymia, the difference between a life organized around the cycling and a life that contains it.

Chapter 10: Cyclothymia and Your Relationships

How many relationships have ended before you could explain what was happening?

Not failed in a straightforward sense. Not ended because of incompatibility or diverging paths or the ordinary reasons that relationships end. Ended in the specific way that cyclothymia relationships tend to end: the other person experienced two versions of you in close succession and did not understand that both versions were the same person in different phases of the same condition. Or you experienced yourself as two different people, capable of intense connection in one phase and genuine absence in another, and could not explain to yourself or to anyone else why the switch happened or when it would switch back.

This is the relational experience of cyclothymia. It is documented, specific, and entirely amenable to change once it is understood.

The Relational Pattern

The relational signature of cyclothymia is produced directly by the cycling itself. During the hypomanic-like phase, the predominant interpersonal experience is one of heightened connection: social energy is high, the other person feels interesting and important, conversation is easy and intense, emotional availability is genuine and substantial. People with cyclothymia in elevated phases are often described by others as charismatic, engaging, and unusually present.

During the depressive phase, the pattern reverses. The same person who was intensely engaged withdraws. Not always dramatically: sometimes the withdrawal is simply a reduction in social initiative, fewer messages, shorter conversations, a disinclination to make plans. But the contrast with the elevated phase can be startling to someone who does not understand what drives it.

Research on cyclothymia's interpersonal consequences confirms what this description suggests: people with cyclothymia tend to pursue intense interpersonal connections during elevated phases and to withdraw into isolation during depressive phases, a pattern that generates a characteristic cycling of closeness and distance that can destabilize relationships over time (Bielecki & Gupta, 2023). The fear of rejection and interpersonal sensitivity that are features of the cyclothymic temperament add to this: the distance of the depressive phase is often misread as indifference or rejection, which amplifies the relational stress.

Interpersonal Sensitivity and Fear of Rejection

Interpersonal sensitivity is one of the defining features of the cyclothymic character, and it operates in both directions of the cycle.

During the elevated phase, the sensitivity is experienced as openness and emotional availability. The other person's responses feel vivid and significant. Connection feels possible and worth pursuing.

During the depressive phase, the sensitivity becomes vulnerability. A delayed reply feels like withdrawal. An ambiguous message reads as criticism. The fear of rejection, which is characteristic of atypical depression and strongly associated with cyclothymia, is most acute during the low phase, making exactly the time when withdrawal might be most understandable also the time when the fear of social rejection is highest. This combination, withdrawing from connection while most afraid of losing it, is one of the more painful features of the depressive phase.

Understanding this pattern does not eliminate it. But naming it shifts its meaning. The withdrawal of the low phase is a symptom of the cycling, not a commentary on the relationship.

How to Talk to a Partner

The conversation about cyclothymia with a partner is almost universally reported as easier to have than anticipated and harder to get started.

The frame that tends to work best is not a diagnostic explanation but a behavioral one. Instead of leading with the diagnosis and its clinical parameters, leading with the observable pattern as the other person has experienced it is more likely to create mutual recognition. "You've probably noticed that I go through periods where I'm very energetic and engaged, and then periods where I seem to pull back. I've got a name for that pattern now, and I want to explain what's happening."

The explanation that follows should cover three things. First, the cycling is a neurobiological pattern, not a choice or a reflection of feelings about the relationship. Second, the withdrawal of the depressive phase is a symptom, not a signal of disconnection. Third, there are things the partner can do that help, and things that do not help, and these are worth agreeing on in advance.

Talking about cyclothymia during a stable or slightly elevated period, rather than in the middle of a low phase, produces better outcomes. During the low phase, the capacity for complex conversation is reduced and the fear of rejection is highest, making the conversation more likely to go badly.

What Helps and What Does Not

Partners who understand the cyclothymia pattern often ask what they can actually do to help. The answer varies between phases.

During the elevated phase, the most helpful partner behavior is calm, non-reactive engagement. Not joining in the elevated energy (which can overstimulate the phase), not dismissing it, but providing a stable presence that neither escalates nor flattens the mood. During elevated phases, gentle reminders about sleep time are more useful than attempts at direct mood intervention.

During the depressive phase, the most helpful behavior is low-demand presence. Not asking for more energy or engagement than exists. Not interpreting the withdrawal as a relationship problem. Practical support, being available without requiring the person to mobilize resources they do not have, is the most valued form of help in the depressive phase. Checking in briefly without expecting a full response.

What consistently does not help, across both phases, is interpreting the phase as a personality statement. "Why are you always like this in the mornings" during a low phase, or "you're impossible to keep up with" during an elevated phase, are understandable responses to a confusing pattern, but they add shame to a situation that is already impairing.

When Relationships End

Not all relationships survive the cycling pattern, and this is a fact worth acknowledging rather than minimizing. Relationships that end before the cyclothymia was diagnosed, or before the partner understood the pattern, are not evidence that cyclothymia makes relationships impossible. They are evidence that cycling without explanation, or with explanation inadequate to the experience, creates a specific and preventable kind of relationship damage.

Processing these losses after a diagnosis often involves a kind of retrospective reframing that can be both clarifying and painful. Understanding that the pattern, rather than a fundamental incompatibility, drove the relationship to end does not restore what ended. It does change the meaning of it and, for many people, reduces the self-blame that accompanied it.

Case 1: Tatum

A composite narrative.

Tatum and their partner had been together for four years when the cyclothymia diagnosis arrived. Their partner, Briar (a pseudonym used with composite permission), described the relationship as "two or three different relationships cycling around inside the same partnership." During Tatum's elevated phases: a relationship that felt exciting and intimate. During the depressive phases: a relationship in which Briar felt alone in the same apartment.

The conversation after the diagnosis was less dramatic than either had anticipated. Tatum explained the cycling pattern and what drove the withdrawal. Briar's first response was: "I thought it was me. I thought you pulled away because you'd decided you weren't interested anymore."

That moment of mutual recognition, that the pattern had been relational damage accumulated across years of misinterpretation, was followed by a practical conversation about what the low phases looked like in behavioral terms and what Briar could usefully do. The agreed protocol was simple: during a low phase, one brief check-in per day (text or five-minute conversation), no requests for plans or decision-making, and a signal phrase (Tatum would say "I'm in a low period") to activate the protocol.

Over the following year, the relationship remained intact through two full cycles. Briar later described the protocol as changing "everything": not because the cycles disappeared, but because they stopped feeling like information about the relationship.

Case 2: Tierney

A composite labeled case.

Background: Tierney, 32, was referred for psychological support following a cyclothymia diagnosis twelve months earlier. The presenting issue was not mood management per se but a pattern of relationship ruptures, three significant relationships ended in the past four years, that Tierney attributed directly to the cyclothymic pattern.

Presentation: Assessment revealed high levels of rejection sensitivity and interpersonal anxiety, particularly in the depressive phase. Tierney described ending relationships preemptively during low phases, predicting rejection before it occurred, as a self-protective strategy that had consistently produced the outcome it was trying to prevent.

Analysis: The interpersonal sensitivity and fear of abandonment characteristic of cyclothymia's depressive phases were functioning as a driver of relationship-ending behavior. The preemptive ending was a misidentified coping strategy: protecting against anticipated rejection by enacting separation first.

Intervention: Interpersonal work in IPSRT focused specifically on the depressive-phase relationship behaviors. Tierney developed an explicit plan for the depressive phase: no relationship-significant decisions during days rated below 4 on the mood chart. Waiting for the phase to shift before acting on the fear of rejection.

Outcome: Over eight months, Tierney did not end a relationship during a depressive phase. The current relationship, described as the most stable of the past decade, was ongoing at the final session.

Teaching Point: Phase-specific behavioral guidelines, particularly around relationship decisions during the depressive phase, can prevent cyclothymia-driven relationship patterns from producing outcomes the person does not actually want.

Closing the Loop

The opening question of this chapter was about relationships that ended before you could explain what was happening.

The answer the chapter offers is this: with a name for the pattern, a partner who understands it, and phase-specific protocols that protect the depressive period from the most costly relational decisions, the relationship damage of cyclothymia is substantially preventable. Not entirely. Not without effort from both people. But the pattern, once named and understood, loses the power it has when it is invisible.

Chapter 11 turns from the relational context of cyclothymia to the professional one: work, career, and managing the productivity cycle in a working life.

Chapter 11: Work Career and Cyclothymia

"I can do anything when I'm up," a person with cyclothymia once said to their IPSRT therapist. "And then I spend three weeks paying for it."

That sentence is a precise description of cyclothymia's occupational signature. The elevated phase produces genuine capability: focused energy, creative output, high productivity, the ability to work long hours without fatigue. The problem is that the elevated phase also produces overcommitment. Projects that get started and then cannot be sustained. Responsibilities accepted enthusiastically that look impossible by Thursday. Emails sent at eleven at night that are regretted by Friday.

The low phase then arrives at exactly the point where the commitments made during the high are most due. The deadline falls during the depressive period. The meeting with the important client is the week after the overscheduled burst. The performance review is the month after the unsustainable commitment.

This is not a character problem. It is a cycling problem. And unlike many aspects of cyclothymia, the work impact is one of the most practically addressable with the right framework.

The Productivity Cycle at Work

The occupational experience of cyclothymia follows the same cycling pattern that governs everything else, but the work environment adds two specific amplifiers.

The first amplifier is the externally imposed schedule. Unlike a social life, which can be adjusted informally to some degree, work has deadlines, meetings, and commitments that do not move around the mood cycle. The mismatch between the cycling of mood and the fixed demands of a work calendar is the primary source of occupational impairment.

The second amplifier is the visibility of the low phase. In a relationship, the depressive withdrawal can be explained or accommodated by someone who understands the condition. In a work environment, missed deadlines, cancelled meetings, and reduced output are visible to colleagues and managers who may have no understanding of cyclothymia and may draw conclusions about reliability or capability.

Clinical guidance from the Merck Manual (2024) specifically recommends jobs with flexible hours for people with cyclothymia, and encourages clinicians to help patients identify careers that are compatible with the variable energy and emotional reactivity that characterize the condition. This is evidence-based clinical advice, not simply a preference. The fit between work environment and cyclothymia's cycle is one of the most modifiable variables in occupational functioning.

The Disclosure Decision

Disclosing a cyclothymia diagnosis to an employer is a decision that involves legal, practical, and relational considerations that vary significantly by jurisdiction, workplace culture, and the nature of the work.

In the UK, the Equality Act 2010 classifies mental health conditions that have a substantial and long-term adverse effect on normal day-to-day activities as disabilities, triggering an employer's duty to make reasonable adjustments. Cyclothymia, with its demonstrated long-term functional impact, is likely to meet this definition for many people, though individual circumstances vary. In the United States, the Americans with Disabilities Act provides similar protections for qualifying conditions.

Disclosure does not mean sharing the diagnosis label. A disclosure conversation can be framed around the functional accommodations being requested without naming cyclothymia specifically: "I have a medical condition that affects my energy levels in a cyclical way. I work most effectively when I can structure my most demanding tasks in the mornings, and I benefit from some flexibility around scheduling." This kind of functional disclosure, focused on what is needed rather than on the diagnostic label, tends to be better received and carries less stigma risk than leading with the diagnosis.

The decision about whether to disclose at all depends on the severity of occupational impact and the nature of the workplace relationship. For people whose cycling is well-managed and whose occupational functioning is maintained, there may be no pressing need for formal disclosure. For people whose cycling is visibly affecting their work, disclosure with a reasonable adjustments conversation may prevent formal performance management that otherwise feels inevitable.

Career Environment Matching

Career environment matching is the deliberate selection or modification of work environments to minimize the mismatch between cyclothymia's variable energy profile and the demands of the role. This is not giving up on ambition. It is a strategic consideration that can substantially reduce the occupational cost of the cycling.

Environments that tend to align better with cyclothymia include those with flexible scheduling, the ability to shift demanding work toward peak-energy periods; project-based structures, where intense effort followed by recovery is a recognized pattern; creative fields, where variable output and intense periods of productivity are culturally accepted; and remote or self-directed work, where the social demands and fixed schedule of an office environment are reduced.

Environments that tend to be higher-risk include those with fixed schedules and high customer-facing demands across all hours; roles requiring sustained, even-paced output with no high-intensity variation; highly managed environments where any deviation from expected performance is immediately visible; and shift work, which carries the circadian disruption risks covered in Chapter 5.

None of this means people with cyclothymia cannot succeed in high-demand, fixed-schedule environments. Many do. The recognition that some environments are structurally more compatible than others is useful information for career planning, not a ceiling.

Building a Work Anchor Routine

The social rhythm therapy principles of Chapter 6 apply directly to the work context. A work anchor routine does for occupational functioning what social rhythm management does for circadian stability: it provides a structured, repeating framework that reduces the impact of mood variation on work output.

A work anchor routine for cyclothymia includes a consistent work start time, even on days when the mood makes starting feel impossible; a defined "minimum effective day" for low-phase periods, a list of the smallest meaningful set of tasks that constitutes an adequate day when full capacity is not available; and a scheduled end to the work day, particularly important during elevated phases when the pull to keep working past midnight is strong.

The minimum effective day concept deserves particular attention because it serves two functions: it provides a concrete target when the low phase is most impairing (the question is no longer "how do I be productive today" but "can I complete these three specific things"), and it prevents the overcommitment that damages the elevated phase by establishing a ceiling as well as a floor.

Managing the Low Phase at Work

The low phase at work is primarily a conservation problem: how to meet the minimum occupational requirements when energy and motivation are substantially below baseline.

Task triage is the most useful low-phase work skill. On the day's task list, the low phase requires identifying which tasks are genuinely time-critical, which can wait for a stable period, and which can be delegated or deprioritized entirely without consequence. The tendency during the low phase to treat all tasks as equally urgent, which generates a kind of paralyzed overwhelm, is itself a symptom. In reality, most tasks can wait.

Communication management during the low phase reduces the social cost of the low's reduced responsiveness. A brief note to key contacts ("I'm in a high-focus period for the next few days and may be slower to respond than usual") is not deceptive, is not a disclosure, and prevents the silence of the low phase from being interpreted as disengagement or unprofessionalism.

Case 1: Umber (Worked Example)

A composite worked example.

Umber worked in a communications role that combined deadline-driven work, client-facing responsibilities, and a requirement to be responsive across most working hours. The cyclothymia diagnosis had arrived eighteen months earlier. The occupational impact had been significant: two formal performance reviews for late work in the past year, both of which had occurred during depressive phases that Umber had not been able to explain to the manager.

Step 1: Mapping the cycle against the work calendar. Umber and their IPSRT therapist reviewed three months of mood chart data alongside the work calendar. The pattern showed that the two performance-review-triggering periods had occurred during depressive phases that had begun approximately two weeks after heavily elevated periods of high output. In each case, the elevated phase had produced significant overcommitment, and the subsequent low had coincided with the delivery deadlines for those commitments.

Step 2: Identifying the overcommitment pattern. The elevated phase's pull to take on new work was identified as the primary occupational risk factor. Umber was accepting new projects during elevated phases without a visible accounting of the delivery timeline relative to the likely subsequent low.

Step 3: The eighteen-day rule. A simple heuristic was developed: any commitment with a delivery date within eighteen days of acceptance required a second review at a stable period before confirmation. This did not prevent Umber from accepting new work during elevated phases. It introduced a forty-eight-hour pause, anchored to a stable mood rating, before confirming.

Step 4: The minimum effective day. A minimum effective day list was defined with the manager, framed as a "focused output" plan rather than a clinical accommodation. On days when full output was not available, three specific tasks constituted an adequate day: reviewing and responding to the most urgent client communications, completing one section of any ongoing project, and updating the project tracking document.

Outcome: Over the following six months, Umber had not received a formal performance review. The elevated phase overcommitment had been reduced by the pause-and-review heuristic. The low phase impact on visible deliverables had been reduced by the minimum effective day structure. Umber described the change as "having a floor and a ceiling at work, instead of just a floor."

Case 2: Vesper

A composite narrative.

Vesper had not disclosed the cyclothymia diagnosis to anyone at work. The organization was large, the culture was not one that Vesper trusted with this kind of information, and the performance impact of the cycling had been, so far, manageable.

The question about disclosure came to a head when a new manager joined the team and began scheduling mandatory Friday afternoon meetings that consistently overlapped with the period Vesper had identified as the most reliably low-energy window of the week. Missing the meetings was not an option. Attending them at baseline capacity was difficult. Attending them during a depressive phase was very nearly impossible.

The IPSRT therapist helped Vesper prepare a disclosure conversation that was functional rather than diagnostic. Vesper asked the manager for a private meeting and said: "I manage a health condition that affects my energy levels in a predictable way across the week. Fridays after three are generally my lowest-capacity time, and I want to flag this so we can discuss whether there's any flexibility in the meeting schedule." The manager moved the meetings to Tuesday morning. No diagnosis was ever named. The accommodation was granted.

Vesper's case illustrates that functional disclosure, framed around what the person needs rather than what the condition is, can produce practical accommodations without requiring the disclosure of diagnostic detail that feels like a privacy risk.

Essential Takeaways

The occupational cost of cyclothymia is real and often substantial. It comes not from incapacity but from the mismatch between the cycling pattern and the fixed demands of most work environments.

Three practical shifts change the picture substantially. First, career environment matching: identifying and moving toward environments where variable energy and flexible scheduling are more possible. Second, the overcommitment guard during elevated phases: a pause mechanism between accepting work and confirming it. Third, the minimum effective day during low phases: a defined floor that prevents the low's paralysis from becoming complete occupational collapse.

The cycling does not stop. The career does not have to stop with it.

Chapter 12: When Cyclothymia Has Company

If you have cyclothymia and something else, you are not unusual. You are the statistical norm.

Cyclothymia is a condition with remarkably high comorbidity rates. Anxiety disorders, attention deficit hyperactivity disorder, substance use disorders, eating disorders, and obsessive-compulsive disorder all co-occur with cyclothymia at rates significantly above base population prevalence (Bielecki & Gupta, 2023). This is not coincidence. The shared neurobiological substrate of emotional dysregulation, circadian vulnerability, and impulsivity creates conditions in which multiple disorders can take root simultaneously.

Understanding the comorbidity pattern matters for two reasons. The first is diagnostic: if a comorbid condition is treated without the underlying cyclothymia being recognized, treatment may be incomplete or counterproductive. The second is treatment sequencing: when cyclothymia and another condition are both present, the order and combination of interventions matters, and cyclothymia management typically needs to be established as a foundation before the comorbid condition receives its own targeted treatment.

Anxiety Disorders

Anxiety is the most common comorbid condition in cyclothymia. The overlap is so consistent that anxiety is sometimes considered a core feature of the cyclothymic temperament rather than a separate comorbid diagnosis.

The anxiety in cyclothymia tends to be most pronounced during the depressive phase, where it presents as an anxious-depressive mixture: low mood, rumination, heightened fear of negative outcomes, and somatic anxiety symptoms (tension headaches, chest tightness, gastrointestinal distress). The elevated phase can also produce anxiety in the form of a pressured, agitated state in which there are too many competing stimuli and demands to process comfortably.

Treatment implications: when both anxiety and cyclothymia are present, the sequencing matters. Treating anxiety with standard anxiolytic approaches, including SSRIs, without addressing the underlying cyclothymia may worsen the cycling. Valproate is particularly useful when anxiety is the dominant comorbid feature, given its anxiolytic properties alongside its mood-stabilizing role. Gabapentin may be helpful for comorbid social anxiety or panic, though its evidence base is modest. CBT for anxiety can be adapted effectively once mood stabilization has been established.

ADHD and Cyclothymia

Attention deficit hyperactivity disorder and cyclothymia share several symptoms that make distinguishing them, and identifying their coexistence, a genuine clinical challenge: both involve inattention, impulsivity, and emotional dysregulation. Both are frequently present in the same person.

Research has documented meaningful overlap between ADHD symptoms and cyclothymia (Youngstrom et al., 2010). The clinical difficulty is that treating ADHD in the context of unrecognized cyclothymia can be counterproductive: stimulant medications, the first-line pharmacological treatment for ADHD, can precipitate or amplify elevated phases in bipolar-spectrum presentations.

The practical sequence is important. When cyclothymia is identified alongside ADHD, mood stabilization should be established first. Stimulant treatment for ADHD, if clinically indicated, is introduced carefully afterward, at low doses, with close mood monitoring. This sequence prevents the stimulant from destabilizing an unsupported cycling system.

Psychologically, the overlapping features of ADHD and cyclothymia require that treatment approaches address both conditions' contributions to the presenting problems. Difficulties with sustained attention may reflect both the distractibility of ADHD and the cycling of cyclothymia's motivational state. The combination warrants careful, phase-aware behavioral strategies that go beyond what either condition's standard treatment provides alone.

Neurodivergent Overlap

The intersection of cyclothymia with other neurodivergent presentations, particularly autism and broader neurodivergent profiles, is an emerging area of clinical attention. Early research has documented higher rates of cyclothymic symptoms in neurodivergent populations and has noted that the emotional dysregulation associated with autism can mask or be masked by cyclothymia's cycling pattern.

The clinical challenge is significant. Emotional dysregulation is a feature of both autism and cyclothymia. Routine-sensitivity is a feature of autism and, through the circadian mechanism, a protective strategy for cyclothymia. Sensory differences in autism may increase stress load and therefore cyclothymia episode risk. The presentations can be difficult to disentangle.

For readers who identify as neurodivergent and have also received a cyclothymia diagnosis, the most useful clinical frame is additive rather than either/or: the neurodivergent profile and the cyclothymia are both present and both relevant to treatment planning. Social rhythm therapy adapted for a neurodivergent sensory and processing profile, and mood stabilization that accounts for the potentially different medication sensitivity profile of autistic individuals, are the two most important clinical considerations.

Substance Use

Substance use comorbidity in cyclothymia is documented at significantly elevated rates compared to the general population (Bielecki & Gupta, 2023). The clinical understanding is primarily self-medication: alcohol reduces anxiety and stimulates social ease during the elevated phase; cannabis modulates the pressured quality of the elevated state; sedatives provide relief from the agitated insomnia that accompanies some elevated phases.

The problem is that all these substances interfere with the circadian system and worsen the cycling pattern they are being used to manage. Alcohol disrupts sleep architecture. Cannabis is inconsistent in its effect on mood and can trigger paranoid depressive states. Sedatives produce rebound wakefulness and rebound anxiety that can tip the system back into an elevated phase.

Addressing substance use in cyclothymia requires acknowledging the genuine function it has been serving before expecting it to stop. The mood stabilization that IPSRT and pharmacotherapy can provide offers a legitimate alternative to the self-medication pattern, but that alternative needs to be in place before the coping mechanism is removed.

Cases: Wren and Xael (Braided)

Both are composite illustrations.

Wren, 29, had been diagnosed with cyclothymia and ADHD simultaneously. Wren's elevated phases were characterized primarily by impulsivity and distractibility rather than elevated mood, making them easy to attribute entirely to ADHD. The depressive phases were clearly not ADHD and had prompted the cyclothymia diagnosis. Wren was started on lamotrigine as the first intervention. Mood stabilization at eight weeks was sufficient to allow a careful trial of low-dose methylphenidate for the ADHD component. The stimulant was titrated slowly, with mood tracking daily throughout the titration. At six months, Wren reported meaningful improvement in sustained attention during stable and slightly elevated periods, without the mood destabilization that an unstabilized stimulant introduction might have produced.

Xael, 33, had cyclothymia alongside generalized anxiety disorder. The anxiety was the presenting complaint, and an SSRI had been tried twice before the cyclothymia was identified. Both SSRI trials had produced short-term improvement in anxiety followed by increased cycling frequency. Once the cyclothymia diagnosis was established, valproate was started as the primary intervention, chosen for its anxiolytic as well as mood-stabilizing properties. Anxiety levels reduced substantially over three months alongside the mood stabilization. The SSRI was not reintroduced.

The braided cases illustrate the principle of addressing cyclothymia as the foundational condition in complex comorbidity presentations: the treatment decisions for the comorbid conditions (ADHD in Wren's case, anxiety disorder in Xael's) became clearer and safer once the cyclothymia was stabilized first.

Case 2: Yael

A composite narrative.

Yael had been drinking heavily for three years by the time the cyclothymia diagnosis arrived. Not alcoholically, in Yael's understanding: no blackouts, no morning drinking, no inability to stop when circumstances demanded it. But a bottle of wine most evenings, and more on weekends, and a genuine sense that without it the evenings were uncomfortable in a way that was hard to specify.

The IPSRT therapist asked about the timing. When in the week was the drinking heaviest? When was it lightest? Yael mapped it onto the mood chart, which showed a consistent pattern: the heaviest drinking occurred on days rated below 4 on the mood scale, and almost never on days rated above 6.

The function of the alcohol was transparent once the map existed: it softened the low phase. It did not eliminate it or cure it. It made the evenings less arid.

The IPSRT process addressed the alcohol use not as an independent problem but as a symptom-management strategy that was causing collateral damage. Lamotrigine, introduced four weeks into treatment, began to reduce the severity of the low phases within six weeks. As the low phases became less arid on their own, the pull to drink through them reduced. Yael had not stopped drinking entirely at the end of treatment, but the volume had halved and the desperate quality of the evening drinking had gone.

"I drink socially now," Yael said at the final session. "Which is how it was supposed to be."

Integration and Synthesis

What is clear: cyclothymia rarely travels alone. Anxiety, ADHD, substance use, and other conditions co-occur at rates that require clinical attention.

What requires ongoing individual assessment: the relative contribution of each condition to the presenting problems, the appropriate sequencing of treatment (cyclothymia stabilization first is the working principle, with adjustments for individual presentations), and the extent to which comorbid conditions respond to cyclothymia-targeted treatment versus requiring their own specific interventions.

The honest position is that comorbid presentations are harder to treat, require more careful sequencing, and often produce messier outcomes than single-condition presentations. This is not a reason for pessimism. It is a reason for clinical precision and realistic expectations, and for working with a clinician who understands the full picture.

Chapter 13: Building Long Term Stability

Stability with cyclothymia does not look the way most people imagine it. The phrase "getting stable" suggests a fixed state, a quieted system, a mood that stops moving. That is not what cyclothymia stability is. The brain with cyclothymia continues to cycle. The circadian vulnerability persists. The emotional reactivity that characterizes the cyclothymic temperament does not disappear with treatment.

What changes, with sustained, well-constructed management, is the relationship to the cycling. Phases become shorter. Amplitude narrows. Recovery between phases is faster. The warning signs become recognizable early enough to respond to them before they reach peak intensity. The accumulated damage, to relationships, career, and self-concept, slows and stops and sometimes reverses. This is a qualitatively different life, even though the cycling continues. It is also what the evidence actually supports expecting.

What the Research Says About Progression

The progression risk in cyclothymia, the possibility that the condition will develop into bipolar I or II, is the figure that most frightens newly diagnosed readers. The estimate that 15 to 50 percent of people with cyclothymia will eventually develop bipolar I or bipolar II disorder is widely cited, frequently without the context that would make it useful (Perugi et al., 2017a).

The context is this: the 15 to 50 percent range reflects variation across studies, and the higher end of that range tends to come from samples of people with more severe cyclothymia or with significant comorbidities, while the lower end comes from broader community samples. More importantly, the progression risk is not static. It is substantially modified by treatment.

The research also shows that many people with cyclothymia maintain a stable cyclothymic course, without progression to higher-threshold bipolar disorder, across decades. This is not a minor point. The framing of cyclothymia as a pre-bipolar condition, inevitable in its escalation, misrepresents the evidence. Progression is a risk to be managed, not a destination that awaits every person with the diagnosis.

What Predicts Progression

The factors associated with increased risk of progression from cyclothymia to bipolar I or II are documented and, importantly, several are modifiable.

Untreated episodes are the strongest predictor of progression, consistent with the kindling model described in Chapter 5. Each cycling episode that occurs without intervention or management reduces the threshold for subsequent episodes. Early, active treatment is therefore the most powerful protection against progression.

Antidepressant use without mood stabilization has been associated with accelerated progression in bipolar-spectrum presentations. The mechanism is the same as the destabilization effect described in Chapter 8: antidepressants activate mood without providing circadian or cycling stabilization, potentially accelerating the kindling process.

Substance use, particularly heavy or regular alcohol use and cannabis use, is associated with increased cycling frequency and severity. Both substances disrupt sleep and circadian anchoring and worsen the cycling pattern in ways that increase progression risk over time.

Sustained sleep disruption beyond the normal cyclothymia profile, particularly patterns of chronic sleep insufficiency, is associated with more severe cycling and greater episode frequency. The circadian pathway to progression operates through sleep.

High life stress with poor social rhythm management creates the conditions for repeated circadian disruption. Major life transitions, chronic occupational stress, and relational instability all carry progression risk through the social zeitgeber pathway.

What Protects Against Progression

The protective factors against cyclothymia progression are, in many cases, the same treatments covered earlier in this guide. The list is not a new set of recommendations: it is a summary of the evidence base the preceding chapters have built.

Active mood stabilizer treatment is the most consistently supported pharmacological protection. Patients maintained on appropriate mood stabilizer regimens show substantially lower rates of progression than untreated patients. The choice of agent matters less than the consistency of treatment: maintained mood stabilization, across years rather than months, is the protective mechanism.

IPSRT and social rhythm management protect against the primary environmental pathway to progression: circadian disruption. Patients who stabilize their social rhythms earlier in treatment show better long-term outcomes in the bipolar-spectrum literature, and the extension of this finding to cyclothymia is supported by the underlying theory and by clinical practice.

Sleep protection is a specific protective behavior within the broader SRT framework. Consistent sleep timing reduces the circadian vulnerability that is the biological mechanism through which environmental stressors translate into episode triggers.

Early phase recognition and response shortens individual episodes and reduces their accumulated biological impact. Mood tracking is the tool that makes early recognition possible. The ability to identify a rising phase before it peaks, and to apply protective measures at that point rather than after the phase has reached its full intensity, may be one of the most practically significant protective factors available.

Avoidance of high-risk substances, particularly alcohol and cannabis, removes two of the most modifiable cycling amplifiers from the clinical picture.

The Kindling Model in Practice

The kindling model predicts that untreated or poorly treated episodes progressively lower the threshold for subsequent episodes. The practical application of this model is: every episode that is managed well, kept shorter through early recognition and protective response, and recovered from without significant life damage, matters. Not just for immediate wellbeing, but for the long-term trajectory of the condition.

This means that the work of cyclothymia management is most effective when it is consistent across the long term rather than crisis-oriented. Implementing protective strategies only during episodes, and abandoning them during stable periods, produces a pattern where the stable periods are not protected from becoming the next episode's precipitant.

Sustained self-management, maintained across stable and unstable periods alike, is what the evidence supports. This is not a comfortable message for people who would prefer to put the condition down when things are going well. It is an accurate one.

Monitoring for Escalation

Even with strong management and good clinical support, cyclothymia can progress. Recognizing the signs of escalation early is the tool that most effectively limits its consequences.

The warning signs that cyclothymia may be escalating include: elevated phases lasting longer than usual or reaching higher peak intensities; depressive phases lasting longer or reaching lower troughs; episodes occurring more frequently or with shorter inter-episode intervals; episodes triggered by progressively smaller stressors or without identifiable stressors; and the introduction of symptoms not previously present, such as paranoid ideation, psychotic features, or impulsivity at a level significantly beyond the person's usual pattern.

Any of these changes warrants contact with a prescriber or mental health clinician. The appropriate response to escalating cycling is a clinical review, not an attempt to self-manage an escalating presentation.

Case 1: Zephyr

A composite labeled case illustrating long-term cyclothymia stability.

Background: Zephyr, 51, was first diagnosed with cyclothymia at age 33, following two decades of untreated cycling that had produced significant relationship and occupational disruption. At diagnosis, Zephyr was started on lamotrigine (titrated to 200mg over three months) and referred for IPSRT.

Long-term course: Over eighteen years of follow-up with two separate clinicians, Zephyr had maintained lamotrigine treatment with one dose adjustment at age 44 following a period of increased cycling associated with a significant bereavement. IPSRT was supplemented by periodic booster sessions during high-stress periods (a career change at 40, a parental illness at 46). Social rhythm management had become, in Zephyr's words, "just how I live rather than something I do."

Presentation at current assessment: Mood chart data across the preceding year showed cycles of fourteen to twenty days in length, with peak ratings between 6 and 7 in the elevated phase and trough ratings between 3 and 4 in the depressive phase. No phase had produced occupational or relational disruption in the past four years. Zephyr described the cycling as "present but peripheral."

Teaching Points:

- Sustained mood stabilizer treatment across decades, with dose adjustments as needed, is associated with progressive stabilization of the cycling pattern.
- IPSRT booster sessions during high-stress transitions protect the social rhythm framework during the periods of highest disruption risk.
- Cyclothymia managed well over the long term can produce a clinical picture where the cycling is present but no longer dominating the person's life.

Case 2: Zennor

A composite narrative.

Zennor had been stable, by any reasonable measure, for three years. The lamotrigine was working. The social rhythm log was a habit. The mood chart showed cycles that were narrow, regular, and non-impairing. Three years is a long time to feel, mostly, fine.

The change arrived slowly, in the way that prodromal signs tend to arrive: not dramatically but incrementally. The elevated-phase peak ratings, which had been sitting at 6.5 for two years, moved to 7.5, then 8.2, across three consecutive cycles. Sleep, which had been protected for three years, started slipping: eleven p.m. became midnight, then twelve-thirty, with no discernible increase in fatigue. Zennor was at a new job, the first in a senior management role, and the demands were absorbing.

Zennor's therapist noticed the chart before Zennor did. "Your peaks are moving," the therapist said at the six-week review. "Three cycles now. And your sleep."

The appointment with the prescriber followed within two weeks. The lamotrigine dose was increased. A temporary return to weekly social rhythm tracking was agreed, with a specific focus on the sleep anchor. The senior role's demands were reviewed for adjustable elements.

The escalation did not continue. The peaks came back down across the following two cycles. The sleep anchor held. The potential progression event was caught, assessed, and interrupted before it reached the threshold that would have produced significant consequences.

"I almost ignored it," Zennor said. "Because I'd been fine for so long. I think I'd started to believe the fine was permanent."

It wasn't permanent. It was managed. Those are not the same thing, and recognizing the distinction, even after three years of stability, was the clinical skill that mattered.

The Larger Picture

There is a question that sits behind everything in this chapter and throughout this guide, and it is worth sitting with rather than answering too quickly.

If cyclothymia is managed well, consistently, across years, with mood stabilization and social rhythm protection and early phase recognition and careful occupational and relational management, what does the life that is possible look like?

Conclusion: Your Personal Stability Plan

The sentence you wrote before reading Chapter 1 is waiting for you now. Whatever you wrote about the moment cyclothymia first made sense as a possibility, read it again.

Some readers find that rereading it produces a kind of cognitive dissonance: the thing they wrote feels less frightening or less mysterious than it did before. The cycling described in that sentence has not changed. What has changed is the framework available to understand it. The biology, the social rhythm theory, the medication landscape, the relational and occupational management strategies, and the long-term prognosis: all of this is now available in a way it was not before this guide.

That is what psychoeducation does. Not eliminate the condition, but remove the darkness that ignorance adds to it.

The Six-Part Personal Stability Plan

The stability plan that follows is not prescriptive. It is a framework. Some parts will apply to your situation more than others. Some parts will need adaptation for your specific comorbidity profile, your medication situation, and your relational and occupational context. Treat it as a starting structure to be modified rather than a rigid protocol to be followed.

Part 1: Your Mood Tracking System. Define how you will track mood going forward. Minimum requirement: twice daily, morning and evening, on a 1 to 10 scale, with sleep duration noted. Decide whether you will use a paper log, a spreadsheet, or an app. Establish a review habit: weekly review of the chart, looking for patterns in the data and for any early warning signs.

Part 2: Your Social Rhythm Anchor Log. Define your five anchor times: target wake time (with acceptable range), target first social contact window, target work start, target dinner window, and target sleep onset. Write them down. Track them for the first month.

Review weekly. Note any week in which a significant disruption occurred and what the rapid return plan was.

Part 3: Your Medication and Therapy Record. Document your current medication (if any), the prescriber's contact details, the monitoring schedule, and any specific instructions about what to do if you notice particular changes. If you are in therapy, document the therapist's contact details and the current focus of treatment. This document is for you, and it is also the document you bring to a clinical appointment or emergency contact.

Part 4: Your Early Warning Sign List. From your mood chart data and your growing knowledge of your own cycling pattern, identify the three to five earliest signs that a phase is beginning. These might include: a specific change in sleep quality before the mood rating changes; a particular quality of thought or speech during the prodromal elevated period; a specific social withdrawal pattern that precedes the depressive phase. Write them down with the corresponding phase they predict. Review and update this list after each cycle.

Part 5: Your Phase-Response Protocol. For each phase, define the response actions. Elevated phase responses might include: protect the sleep anchor, postpone major decisions for 48 hours, activate the minimum effective day work plan, initiate the relationship phase-communication protocol with your partner. Depressive phase responses might include: activate the low-phase work plan, notify the prescriber if the phase extends beyond your usual duration, maintain anchor wake time.

Part 6: Your Support Network Map. Identify the people in your life who know about the cyclothymia diagnosis and who can be contacted during a difficult phase. For each person, note what kind of support they are best positioned to provide. One person may be the practical helper during a depressive phase; another may be the partner who holds the relationship phase-communication protocol; another may be the prescriber or therapist who should be contacted if escalation is suspected. Having the network mapped means you do not have to construct it from scratch during the period when constructing anything is hardest.

The Maintenance Mindset

The most important shift in the long-term management of cyclothymia is from a crisis orientation to a maintenance orientation. A crisis orientation responds to episodes as they arrive, mobilizing protective strategies at peak symptom intensity. A maintenance orientation maintains the protective strategies across stable and unstable periods alike, preventing the crisis from reaching its full intensity.

This requires accepting that the social rhythm log, the mood tracking, and the anchor time protection are permanent features of a well-managed life with cyclothymia, not temporary interventions to be dropped when things improve. The things improve because the interventions are in place. Dropping the interventions removes the conditions that produced the improvement.

This is not a life sentence of effort. These practices, maintained consistently, become habit. They become how you live rather than something you do. Zephyr's description of social rhythm management after eighteen years was exactly this: "just how I live."

When to Seek Urgent Help

Several situations warrant contact with a mental health clinician or emergency services rather than self-management.

Contact your prescriber or mental health clinician if: cycling is escalating across multiple consecutive cycles; phases are lasting longer or reaching higher or lower intensities than your usual pattern; phases are beginning without identifiable triggers in a pattern that has not been seen before; a medication change appears to be worsening cycling; or you are experiencing symptoms not previously part of your cycling pattern.

Contact emergency services or a crisis line if: you are experiencing suicidal thoughts with intent or plan; you are experiencing psychotic symptoms (hearing voices, paranoid beliefs, loss of contact with reality); or you are in a state that feels unsafe to manage alone.

What Earns Its Place

The sentence you wrote before reading Chapter 1 probably described confusion. A long diagnostic journey. An experience of being inside something you couldn't name. A moment of recognition when the word cyclothymia finally arrived.

The question that opened the conclusion chapter of this guide was about what life looks like when cyclothymia is well managed. The answer is that it looks like a life. Not a life without cycling. Not a life defined by a diagnosis. A life that contains the cycling without being organized around it. A life in which the phases are recognizable, the responses are practiced, the support network is real, and the accumulated damage, to relationships, to career, to the sense of self, has slowed and, in significant measures, stopped.

That life is possible. The tools to build it are in your hands.

Appendix A: DSM-5-TR Criteria for Cyclothymic Disorder

The following is a plain-language summary of the DSM-5-TR diagnostic criteria for Cyclothymic Disorder (309.89 / F34.0). This is not a verbatim reproduction of the DSM-5-TR. For clinical use, consult the source text.

Criterion A: For at least two years (one year in children and adolescents), the person has experienced numerous periods with hypomanic symptoms that do not meet the full criteria for a hypomanic episode, and numerous periods with depressive symptoms that do not meet the full criteria for a major depressive episode.

Criterion B: During the two-year period (one year in children and adolescents), the hypomanic and depressive periods have been present for at least half the time, and the person has not been without symptoms for more than two months at a time.

Criterion C: The criteria for a major depressive, manic, or hypomanic episode have never been met.

Criterion D: The symptoms in Criterion A are not better explained by schizoaffective disorder, schizophrenia, schizophreniform disorder, delusional disorder, or other specified or unspecified schizophrenia spectrum and other psychotic disorder.

Criterion E: The symptoms are not attributable to the physiological effects of a substance (e.g., a drug of abuse, a medication) or another medical condition.

Criterion F: The symptoms cause clinically significant distress or impairment in social, occupational, or other important areas of functioning.

Appendix B: 30-Day Mood Tracking Chart

Instructions: Rate your mood and energy twice daily (morning and evening) on a scale of 1 to 10, where 1 is the lowest you have been, 5 is neutral, and 10 is the highest you have been. Record hours of sleep in the sleep column. Note any significant events in the notes column.

Date	Morning Mood	Morning Energy	Evening Mood	Evening Energy	Sleep (hours)	Notes
Day 1						
Day 2						
Day 3						
Day 4						
Day 5						
Day 6						
Day 7						
Day 8						
Day 9						
Day 10						
Day 11						
Day 12						
Day 13						
Day 14						
Day 15						
Day 16						
Day 17						

Date	Morning Mood	Morning Energy	Evening Mood	Evening Energy	Sleep (hours)	Notes
Day 18						
Day 19						
Day 20						
Day 21						
Day 22						
Day 23						
Day 24						
Day 25						
Day 26						
Day 27						
Day 28						
Day 29						
Day 30						

After 30 days, review your chart. Look for: the typical peak and trough ratings, the length of elevated and depressive periods, and any consistent relationship between sleep and mood the following day.

Appendix C: Social Rhythm Weekly Planner

Target Anchor Times (set once, review monthly):

- Wake time target: _______ (acceptable range: _______ to _______)
- First social contact target window: _______ to _______
- Work/activity start target: _______
- Dinner target window: _______ to _______
- Sleep onset target: _______

Weekly Tracking Grid:

Anchor Activity	Mon	Tue	Wed	Thu	Fri	Sat	Sun
Wake time (actual)							
Within target? (Y/N)							
First social contact							
Within target? (Y/N)							
Work start (actual)							
Within target? (Y/N)							
Dinner time (actual)							
Within target? (Y/N)							
Sleep onset (actual)							

Anchor Activity	Mon	Tue	Wed	Thu	Fri	Sat	Sun
Within target? (Y/N)							

Weekly review notes: Which anchors were most consistently protected? Which were most disrupted? What was the relationship between anchor disruption and mood ratings that week?

Appendix D: Medication Conversation Guide

The following questions can help structure a productive conversation with your prescriber about medication for cyclothymia.

Before the appointment, prepare:

1. A summary of your mood chart data (two to three months is useful if available).
2. A complete medication history: what you have taken, the dose, how long, and what the effect was.
3. A brief description of your current cycling pattern: how long are your elevated phases, how long are your depressive phases, and which is more impairing?

Questions to ask your prescriber:

- Based on my cycling pattern, which medication would you recommend as a first choice and why?
- What is the relationship between cyclothymia and antidepressants, and how does this affect your recommendation?
- What dose will we start at, and what is the titration schedule?
- What specific effects should I be tracking to assess whether the medication is working?
- What side effects should I be aware of, and which would warrant contacting you?
- How long before we expect to see a meaningful effect?
- What monitoring will be required (blood tests, etc.) and how often?
- If the first medication does not produce sufficient response, what would be the next step?
- Are there interactions between this medication and any other medications or supplements I currently take?

- What is the plan if I want to change or stop this medication in the future?

Appendix E: Resources and Further Reading

Books

Price, P. Y. (2005). *The cyclothymia workbook: Learn how to manage your mood swings and lead a balanced life*. New Harbinger Publications. [The only other dedicated consumer book on cyclothymia. Now 20 years old but contains useful CBT exercises.]

Frank, E. (2005). *Treating bipolar disorder: A clinician's guide to interpersonal and social rhythm therapy*. Guilford Press. [Clinical guide to IPSRT, primarily for practitioners but accessible to motivated readers.]

Miklowitz, D. J. (2010). *The bipolar disorder survival guide: What you and your family need to know*. Guilford Press. [Bipolar I/II focused but contains substantial IPSRT and social rhythm content applicable to cyclothymia.]

Online Community

r/cyclothymia on Reddit provides an active peer support community. Search terms: cyclothymia, cyclothymic disorder. Note that community content is not clinically supervised; use with appropriate critical evaluation.

Clinical and Professional Resources

National Institute of Mental Health (NIMH): bipolar spectrum resources at nimh.nih.gov

Mind (UK): mind.org.uk, bipolar and mood disorder resources

Rethink Mental Illness (UK): rethink.org

Depression and Bipolar Support Alliance (DBSA, US): dbsalliance.org

Appendix F: Early Warning Sign Worksheet

Use the chart below to document your personal early warning signs for each phase. These signs may be behavioral, cognitive, physical, or interpersonal. Review after each cycle to refine the list.

My Early Warning Signs for the Elevated Phase:

My Early Warning Signs for the Depressive Phase:

Phase-Response Protocol Summary:

When I notice elevated phase early warning signs, I will:

1. ______________________________________

2. ______________________________________

3. ______________________________________

When I notice depressive phase early warning signs, I will:

1. ______________________________________

2. ______________________________________

3. ______________________________________

Appendix G: Glossary of Key Terms

Anchor activities: The five daily activities whose timing is most important for circadian stability in social rhythm therapy: wake time, first social contact, work start, dinner time, and sleep onset.

Bipolar spectrum: The range of mood disorders with shared biological and genetic features, extending from cyclothymia through bipolar II to bipolar I.

Circadian rhythm: The body's internal approximately 24-hour biological clock, which regulates sleep, alertness, hormone secretion, and many other functions.

Cyclothymia (cyclothymic disorder): A mood disorder characterized by recurring periods of hypomanic and depressive symptoms, neither reaching the full threshold of a hypomanic episode or major depressive episode, persisting for at least two years in adults.

DSM-5-TR: The Diagnostic and Statistical Manual of Mental Disorders, Fifth Edition, Text Revision (2022), the primary diagnostic classification system for mental health conditions in the United States.

Euthymia: A state of stable, relatively normal mood; the term used in clinical contexts to describe periods of stable mood between episodes in mood disorders.

Hypomania: A state of elevated, expansive, or irritable mood with increased activity or energy, less severe than full mania, lasting at least four consecutive days in a diagnosable hypomanic episode. In cyclothymia, hypomanic-like periods exist but do not meet the full hypomanic episode criteria.

IPSRT (Interpersonal and Social Rhythm Therapy): A psychotherapy for bipolar-spectrum disorders that combines social rhythm management with interpersonal therapy, developed by Ellen Frank and colleagues.

Kindling: The theoretical process by which repeated mood episodes progressively lower the threshold for subsequent episodes, making each episode easier to trigger.

Lamotrigine: An anticonvulsant medication used as a mood stabilizer, particularly effective for the depressive component of bipolar-spectrum disorders.

Lithium: A mood stabilizer used across the bipolar spectrum with the longest evidence base of any mood-active medication.

Prodrome: The early warning period before a mood episode reaches full intensity, during which intervention is most effective.

Social zeitgeber: An external social time cue (mealtime, social contact, work schedule) that anchors the body's internal circadian clock.

Social rhythm therapy (SRT): The practical application of the social zeitgeber theory to stabilize mood through consistent daily routines.

Valproate (valproic acid, divalproex sodium): An anticonvulsant medication used as a mood stabilizer, particularly useful when anxiety or mixed states are prominent.

Zeitgeber: From German, meaning "time giver"; an external environmental or social cue that synchronizes the body's biological clock.

References

Akiskal, H. S., Djenderedjian, A. H., Rosenthal, R. H., & Khani, M. K. (1977). Cyclothymic disorder: Validating criteria for inclusion in the bipolar affective group. *American Journal of Psychiatry*, *134*(11), 1227-1233.

Akiskal, H. S., & Pinto, O. (1999). The evolving bipolar spectrum: Prototypes I, II, III, and IV. *Psychiatric Clinics of North America*, *22*(3), 517-534.

American Psychiatric Association. (2022). *Diagnostic and statistical manual of mental disorders* (5th ed., text rev.). American Psychiatric Association Publishing.

Bielecki, J. E., & Gupta, V. (2023). Cyclothymic disorder. In *StatPearls*. StatPearls Publishing.

Cleveland Clinic. (2022). *Cyclothymia (cyclothymic disorder): Symptoms and treatment*. Cleveland Clinic.

Ehlers, C. L., Frank, E., & Kupfer, D. J. (1988). Social zeitgebers and biological rhythms: A unified approach to understanding the etiology of depression. *Archives of General Psychiatry*, *45*(10), 948-952.

Fava, G. A., Rafanelli, C., Tomba, E., Guidi, J., & Grandi, S. (2011). The sequential combination of cognitive behavioral treatment and well-being therapy in cyclothymic disorder. *Psychotherapy and Psychosomatics*, *80*(3), 136-143.

Frank, E., Kupfer, D. J., Thase, M. E., Mallinger, A. G., Swartz, H. A., Fagiolini, A. M., Grochocinski, V., Houck, P., Scott, J., Thompson, W., & Monk, T. (2005). Two-year outcomes for interpersonal and social rhythm therapy in individuals with bipolar I disorder. *Archives of General Psychiatry*, *62*(9), 996-1004.

Frank, E., Swartz, H. A., & Kupfer, D. J. (2000). Interpersonal and social rhythm therapy: Managing the chaos of bipolar disorder. *Biological Psychiatry*, *48*(6), 593-604.

Harvey, A. G., Talbot, L. S., & Gershon, A. (2009). Sleep disturbance in bipolar disorder across the lifespan. *Clinical Psychology: Science and Practice*, *16*(2), 256-277.

Jacobsen, F. M. (1993). Low-dose valproate: A new treatment for cyclothymia, mild rapid cycling disorders, and premenstrual syndrome. *Journal of Clinical Psychiatry*, *54*(6), 229-234.

Merck Manual Professional Edition. (2024). *Cyclothymic disorder*. Merck & Co.

Miklowitz, D. J., & Johnson, S. L. (2006). The psychopathology and treatment of bipolar disorder. *Annual Review of Clinical Psychology*, *2*, 199-235.

Perugi, G., Hantouche, E., & Vannucchi, G. (2017a). Diagnosis and treatment of cyclothymia: The "primacy" of temperament. *Current Neuropharmacology*, *15*(3), 372-379.

Perugi, G., Vannucchi, G., & Mazzarini, L. (2017b). The treatment of cyclothymia. In A. F. Carvalho & E. Vieta (Eds.), *The treatment of bipolar disorder: Integrative clinical strategies and future directions* (pp. 123–137). Oxford University Press.

Post, R. M. (1992). Transduction of psychosocial stress into the neurobiology of recurrent affective disorder. *American Journal of Psychiatry*, *149*(8), 999-1010.

Price, P. Y. (2005). *The cyclothymia workbook: Learn how to manage your mood swings and lead a balanced life*. New Harbinger Publications.

Ree, M. J., & Harvey, A. G. (2004). Investigating safety behaviours in insomnia: The development and initial validation of the sleep-related behaviours questionnaire. *Behaviour Research and Therapy*, *42*(9), 1007-1022.

Scott, J., Etain, B., Miklowitz, D., Crouse, J. J., Carpenter, J., Marwaha, S., Smith, D., Merikangas, K., & Hickie, I. (2022). A systematic review and meta-analysis of sleep and circadian rhythms in euthymic bipolar disorder. *Neuroscience and Biobehavioral Reviews*, *135*, 104585.

Suppes, T., & Dennehy, E. B. (2002). Evidence-based long-term treatment of bipolar II disorder. *Journal of Clinical Psychiatry*, *63*(Suppl. 10), 29-33.

Youngstrom, E. A., Arnold, L. E., & Frazier, T. W. (2010). Bipolar and ADHD comorbidity: Both artifact and outgrowth of shared mechanisms. *Clinical Psychology: Science and Practice*, *17*(4), 350-359.

www.ingramcontent.com/pod-product-compliance
Lightning Source LLC
LaVergne TN
LVHW050824061126
851857LV00012B/966